Great Britons On Success

The process of writing this book
and the motto of the RAF, its inspiration:

Per ardua ad astra

Great Britons On Success

Timely and timeless winning ways

ALAN COPPIN

a co-publication

Kingsham Press
www.akdpress.com

RAFBF
THE HEART
OF THE RAF FAMILY
www.rafbf.org

First published in 2009
by Kingsham Press and Royal Air Force Benevolent Fund

Kingsham Press
Oldbury Complex
Marsh Lane
Easthampnett
Chichester, West Sussex
PO18 0JW
United Kingdom

Royal Air Force Benevolent Fund
67 Portland Place
London
W1B 1AR
Registered Charity No. 1081009 (England and Wales)
Registered in Scotland as Charity No. SCO38109

Typeset in Palatino

Printed and bound in Great Britain by MPG Biddles Ltd, King's Lynn, Norfolk

ISBN: 978-1-904235-64-4

British Library Cataloging in Publication Data
A catalogue record of this book is available from the British Library

Coppin, Alan

Acknowledgements

Thank you to Gaynor, my wife, for putting up with me for much of 2008, whilst I have been working on this project and, as ever, for being my constant support, my sounding board and my inspiration. Whatever limited success I have achieved in my life is actually down to her.

Thank you to the RAF Benevolent Fund and in particular Dean Benton for agreeing to back this venture. My special thanks to Loretta Allen, who works for the Fund, and who has provided not only secretarial support but wise counsel.

Thank you to the 67 great Britons who have contributed entries to the book – it is through their benevolence that, hopefully, significant sums will be raised for the charity.

Thank you to the experts on success who have allowed me to use their words in the text and for the writers who have given copyright permission. Whilst every effort has been made to seek permission to include excerpts and attribution, any omission as such is regretted and will be rectified on notice.

Thank you to friends and colleagues and family who have helped me and in particular Terry Sampson, David Payne, my son, Ed whose comments on the draft manuscript were insightful and were fully incorporated in the final text. Thank you also to Maria Teresa Campos Partera for her formatting expertise.

Finally, thank you to Anand Kumar of the publishers, Kingsham Press, for bringing this project to fruition and for his kindness and generosity in matching my royalty donation to the RAF Benevolent Fund.

About Alan Coppin

Alan Coppin has run iconic British institutions such as Historic Royal Palaces and Wembley Stadium and chaired the charities, The Prince's Foundation and 'Include'. He is currently a non-executive director of three public companies, of Air Command (RAF) and is a Patron of the Windsor Leadership Trust. Alan is co-author of *Timeless Management* (Palgrave, 2002). He has donated his royalties to the RAF Benevolent Fund.

Contents

Foreword

First and foremost, I would like to take this opportunity to thank Alan Coppin for the outstanding generosity and support he has shown to the RAF Benevolent Fund by undertaking this project. I know the considerable time and effort which has gone into researching and writing this book which will play a propitious part in helping us to commemorate the 90th anniversary of the RAFBF.

One of the entries in this book is about Sir Winston Churchill who played a key role in the history of the Benevolent Fund. It was his historic radio appeal to the nation in 1951 on behalf of the RAFBF, which gave the charity its current motto: **'*The Debt We Owe*'**. In that speech, Sir Winston referred to the Battle of Britain as 'our finest hour'. It is that same spirit of determination and success which our nation and people have displayed time and again throughout history, which Alan has captured so vividly in this inspirational book.

In keeping with the theme of this book, I would like to suggest that the Royal Air Force Benevolent Fund itself has been extremely successful in delivering vital welfare services to veterans of both World Wars and the National Service veterans, as well as to a new generation of younger members of the RAF family that are facing very different challenges generated by modern warfare and the demands of our contemporary society.

Whether it be an injured serviceman whose home has been adapted for wheelchair access through a Benevolent Fund grant; a serving woman who is able to access affordable childcare through one of the 26 childcare centres funded by the charity; or an ex-Serviceman and his wife who have found their way out of debt by using the RAFBF-funded Money and Benefits Advice Service – the Fund is here to ensure that every member of the RAF family has access to the support they need.

In looking forward, we will do our utmost to ensure that we maintain the tradition of the RAF family by looking out for each other and never forgetting to repay the 'Debt We Owe'. This book is an opportune and inspirational reminder to us to redouble our efforts. But it also provides insights on timely and timeless winning ways that will be of value to us all, whether as individuals, family members or employees across sectors.

Air Marshal Sir Robert Wright KBE AFC FRAeS FCMI
Controller of the Royal Air Force Benevolent Fund

Preface

The inspiration for this book is the men and women who serve in the Royal Air Force. In late 2007, I was appointed a non executive director of Air Command, a role which brought me into direct contact with these people. Part of my induction involved visiting six RAF stations and it was during these visits that I met a large number of personnel, including over 200 in small meetings. What struck me, as someone with no previous connection to the military, was the professionalism, dedication, bravery and selflessness of the people I met and how successful the RAF was and had been since its inception in 1918, through every conflict from the Battle of Britain to present-day operations in Iraq and Afghanistan. From my experience in the commercial sector, I was able to make some comparison between the operational capability and performance of the RAF with private sector companies. As a result of that exercise I formed the view that the RAF is undoubtedly a world class organisation. Furthermore, the ethos of its people seems to be 'Country, Duty' followed some way by 'Self' and this really hit me when I have had exposure to the rather different 'Me Me Me' credo of some parts of the commercial sector.

And yet, as I toured the Air Force stations I did not get the impression that the people who serve in the RAF, including senior officers, realised how successful they were and, indeed, how much they were valued. Of course, this form of modesty may well be a British rather than just an organisational trait, but it seems to me far more advanced in the RAF than in other businesses I have been associated with.

At about this time I learned that 2008 is the 90th anniversary of the formation of the RAF and 2009 the anniversary of the founding of the RAF Benevolent Fund, the charity which supports the RAF family. In some way I made a connection between these events and the success concept and the idea of writing a book themed on success, to benefit the RAF charity and therefore the people from the RAF family who serve or have served their country so selflessly was conceived.

Coincidentally, I had just come across Einstein's formula for success:

$$A = x + y + z$$

where A is success, x is work, y is play and z is knowing when to keep your mouth shut! I thought it would be interesting to find out the success formulae of great modern Britons, the good and the great and unsung heroes, and use this as a main theme of the book. It would also give the entrants themselves the opportunity to show support for the RAF by donating written pieces for the book. That was how Chapter 2 was born.

In order to properly interpret the entries kindly provided for this chapter, I thought it might help to provide an account on the methodology I used to identify potential contributors. This was not a scientific exercise. It simply involved undertaking a range of fairly obvious and basic research including: surfing the internet; checking databases; reading through reference books such as *Who's Who*, *The Guinness Book of World Records* and biographies and autobiographies; finding out winners of awards events such as the Nobel Prize, the Academy Awards and the Greatest Briton annual award; and also, importantly, consulting friends and colleagues and reading contemporary material, especially UK newspapers and magazines.

The list I subsequently prepared was intended to represent the full spectrum of British society, not just the good and the great but also, importantly, a number of unsung heroes. I tried to minimise the number of people who are famous for just being famous: members of the celebrity cult. The entrants who are actually featured in Chapters 2 and, indeed, Chapter 3 are not there because they are my personal preferences but, rather, they are included because they resulted from my research and, of course, because they were kind enough to reply to my approaches.

Inevitably, some people were too busy – I had quite an extensive exchange of emails with one well known individual's representative who, I think with a straight face, told me the noble Lord was too tied up to spend a minute or so choosing some inspirational words. But these were minor irritations and they were largely overcome simply by including publicly available quotations and insights of individuals I wanted to feature in Chapter 4.

As to methodology, once I had generated the list, I simply wrote to the people on it requesting a written entry to include their formula for success together with any explanation and tips for success. The sheet setting out the preferred entry format which I sent out is set out in the Appendix. What I also offered them in a covering letter was complete editorial control over their 'piece' and so what you will find in Chapter 2 is a collection of individual entries, mostly with success formulae, some with supporting script and some without. The text was totally prepared by the respondents and so, for example, Michael Winner's description of his OBE as 'offered but declined' is his humour, not mine. The reason I designed the book in this way is because I thought that you, the reader, might actually find the actual format of the entries (in addition to their content) insightful.

An interesting finding from the research phase of this anthology is that there appears to be a reluctance on the part of many successful Britons to discuss success, either their own, or the concept more generally: it is just not British! This bears out research undertaken by the Royal Society of Arts in 2004 which identified modesty as a fundamental British characteristic. Thankfully, 67 contributors readily provided entries and in the process put aside their own misgivings for the greater good. I am truly grateful to those people for their time and their generosity of spirit.

The scope of the book expanded when I considered it would be interesting to compare the entries of contemporary Britons with deduced pieces from historic Britons and so I selected ten characters who featured in the 2002 BBC poll (voted on by over 1 million people) of *100 Greatest Britons*. These are featured in Chapter 5. In an attempt to keep the book light and true to its 'anthology' format, I also added chapters with short insights and quotations on success by living and historic figures (Chapters 4 and 6 respectively). Again I considered it would be interesting to compare the style and content between different generations.

Chapter 1 attempts to shed some light on the definition of 'success' (I took account of the breadth of the definition set out in the chapter in selecting entrants for the book) and the concluding chapter (Chapter 7) tries to give some further tips on alternative approaches to achieving success.

In conducting the research there is relatively little published material that I have found originating in the United Kingdom. There is no such diffidence about writing about success on the other side of the Atlantic – the self improvement and business shelves of bookshops are filled with books on success in the USA, where I stayed whilst writing part of the book, and so I have used them as reference sources in compiling Chapters 1 and 7.

A key aim of this anthology is to raise funds for the RAF family who serve our country so selflessly. My royalties are donated to the Benevolent Fund and I am grateful to the publisher for matching my donation.

A secondary objective of the book is to provide a comprehensive reference source on the topic of success from a British perspective as this does not appear to have been done before. Indeed this book is, arguably, the most comprehensive assembly of British views on success ever written.

Why just British? This was not because of any xenophobic motive on my part but because it seemed appropriate given the fundraising motive behind the book of helping people who have served in the British Forces. Furthermore, in an age of increasing globalisation, our sense of national identity can sometimes appear to be under threat and perhaps, in some small way, this book might help to redress the balance. Also, the time seemed right to celebrate British success given the public mood undoubtedly heightened by events such as the performance of Team GB and the Paralympics squad at the Beijing Olympics.

The focus on a British perspective enabled me, when making my selection of people to include in the book, to bear in mind the four British traits which the Royal Society of Arts identified in their 2004 work on the perceptions of British characteristics: adaptability, modesty, sense of humour, and strength and determination.

The lay-out I have chosen for the book leaves a great deal of white space around a large number of the entries, particularly in Chapters 4 and 6. I appreciate that this is an unusual and, perhaps on the face of it, an extravagant design choice. The white space is, however, intended to encourage calm consideration and reflection, allowing us the time to digest, learn from and enjoy the ideas, thoughts and insights that the offerings convey, rather than rush mentally from piece to piece.

Above all else I hope that the result of my nine months or so of (admittedly enjoyable) part-time work is of interest and amusement and perhaps even some use to you the reader – please let me know how successful I have been in this aim by emailing me at alancoppin@gbos.co.uk

1
What is Success?

For the residents of a suburb of Perth in Western Australia, *Success* is their home; likewise, for the inhabitants of towns in Arkansas, Missouri and New Hampshire in the United States of America. Some people incarcerated by the Australian state in the late 19th century had a strange experience of *Success* as it was their prison ship. Many sailors in the Royal Navy and Royal Australian Navy served on a number of ships which were also called *Success*. The word had completely different associations for the American girl group 'The Weather Girls' who used it to name their first album (1983) and to Australian singer Dannii Minogue as it was the title of one of her singles, recorded in 1991. For the employees of a Japanese computer game business it is their company name. Budding entrepreneurs in the USA consult *Success* magazine for ideas on how to get rich and budding French models send in their portfolios to the *Success* model agency in Paris.

But most people when wishing to answer the question 'What is Success?' would probably refer to a source such as the *Oxford English Dictionary*:

> **Success**, *noun*. the accomplishment of an aim or purpose; the gaining of fame, wealth or social status; a person or thing that achieves success.

However, in undertaking the research for this book, I have found that this dictionary definition does not fully answer the question – there appears to be literally hundreds of different interpretations of the noun and also, perhaps, some confusion between accomplishment and success. For the purpose of this debate, accomplishment is where you have engaged in the task or action that you attempted, and have obtained the desired results. It is based on what was expected, and what results were achieved. This is a daily happening in the world and marketplace. People accomplish things all day long, but would not really define such achievements as *Success*. The concept of success is something rather different. To most people it is when you have an ongoing string of accomplishments (that can be related to business matters, social or leisure issues wealth, health, charitable efforts, or life generally) that, when put together, add up to a major achievement.

As J. Pincott points out in the book she edited, entitled *Success* (Random House, 2005):

> 'Almost every person has his or her own definition of success – and many of these definitions are anything but definite. It's worthwhile to think about what success means to you and what it means to others. And it's up to you to decide if you want the latter to influence the former. ... And, in the most general sense, success may be defined by the quality of life you lead and the model you set for others.'

This point was developed further by Jerry Porras, Stewart Emery and Mark Thompson in their book *Success Built to Last: Creating a Life that Matters* (Wharton School Publishing, 2007). They contend that the:

> 'current definition [of success] is a potentially toxic prescription for your life and work. It is a description that makes you feel more like a failure than a success if it's the standard against all meaning in your life is measured ... the real definition is a life and work that brings personal fulfilment and lasting relationships and makes a difference in the world in which we live.'

The vast majority of the people I consulted in my research phase had never quite thought about success in these terms and, initially, responded to my quizzing on the topic by responding that success is defined primarily in terms of career and the accumulation of money or fame. They eventually widened the description to include happiness, fulfilment (in work and family), sharing love of family and friends and, of course, good health.

Obviously, these elements may well have different weightings – 58% of people polled in a survey by the aforementioned *Success* magazine cited 'good health' as the most important element of success for them.

The best selling author Deepak Chopra stressed the importance of deeper attributes of success and particularly the spiritual element of the definition when he wrote:

> 'Success in life could be defined as the continued expansion of happiness and the progressive realisation of worthy goals. There are many aspects to success; material wealth is only one component. Moreover, success is a journey, not a destination. Material

abundance, in all its expressions, happens to be one of those things that make the journey more enjoyable. But success also includes good health, energy and enthusiasm for life, fulfilling relationships, creative freedom, emotional and psychological stability, a sense of well-being and peace of mind. Even with the experience of all these things, we will remain unfulfilled unless we nurture the seeds of divinity inside us... When we begin to experience our life as the miraculous expression of divinity – not occasionally, but all of the time – then we will know the true meaning of success.'

On the other hand, Jim Collins set out a more corporate and corporeal viewpoint in his book *Good to Great* where he argued that it in order to have a meaningful life it is necessary to have meaningful work and that assessing this success in itself was not enough.

Whether it is about a meaningful life, meaningful work, luck, family and cultural experiences etc, it is obvious, as several of the entries have made clear and echoed in Malcolm Gladwell's (2008) new book *Outliers: The Story of Success*, that success is contingent upon hard work and a drive to achieve mastery through practice.

In the pages that follow, many of the great Britons featured define or allude to what success is to them – hopefully, with the above thoughts this will help you to clarify your own thinking.

As to why it is important to be clear about our own personal view of success, Dr Robert Holden in his book *Success Intelligence* (Hodder and Stoughton, 2005), sets out a powerful argument for us each developing our own definition:

'"What is success?" This question is so important, I believe that how well you answer this question determines how well you will live your life. Yet, many people tell me that they are too busy doing, busy chasing, busy working to have time to formulate clearly their thoughts about success. Only very rarely have I met anyone who has written a personal definition of success. It seems most people prefer to chase something they haven't thought about. ... Life isn't just about "getting there", it is also about "being here" and enjoying your journey. Therefore, when I ask people "What is success?" I want to make sure they are using measures for both the journey and the end. Ultimately, the journey is the end, anyway.'

Success is not a concept just applied to individuals or even to teams or organisations; it can be a great unifying ideal. As was pointed out by the

'Comment' column in the *Daily Mail* newspaper following the Team GB performance at the Beijing Olympics:

> '… Success in Beijing doesn't belong to one part of the country, but to all of us. This is Team GB, with athletes from every corner of this United Kingdom. We have shown we are capable of remarkable things when we stand together. Let's not forget that.'

In the same newspaper Stephen Glover pointed to the importance of how this success was achieved, when he referred to the British team's attitude:

> '… there was an innocent joy in success, and an absence of vanity. Sport, it seems, can entail the pursuit of excellence without the taint of over-inflated egos. What has struck me about our medal winners –and no doubt those of other nations – has been their lack of boastfulness, and their pride in their team's, and, by extension, their country's success.'

These points of view might resonate with you and you might like to bear them in mind when reading the rest of this book. Or you might prefer to take a much lighter approach such as that of Terry Sampson, a friend of mine for over 30 years, who when I asked him for his personal definition of success replied:

> 'Success is getting to the toilet before you pee your pants!'

2
Success Formulae of Contemporary Britons

The following entries were provided in response to the guide sheet set out in the Appendix, of people prepared to put their heads above the modesty parapet and provide their own formulae for success.

Peter Alliss

Golfer, television commentator, golf course architect, writer

Find out about yourself; look in the mirror; what do you see? Learn to do the simple things in life well. Try to improve your diction and vocabulary; don't be put off by people who imagine you're getting 'ideas above your station' or are becoming a snob; believe me it can pay handsome dividends. It's up to you.

Success is very illusive. On examination you will find there are hundreds of levels of 'success'. Personally, I didn't understand its meaning until I'd reached the age of about 30, although I had initial success in the world of golf from the age of 21. Why? Well in those far off days, the only thing most people of my age were concerned with, particularly those who had no academic qualifications, was how to make a living. My father, Percy Alliss, was a well respected golf professional in the 1920s and '30s, having served in the first World War with the Argyll and Sutherland Highlanders, and on repatriation got his first job in the world of professional golf at the Royal Porthcawl Golf Club in south Wales. From there he went to Clyne, but the big move happened when he became the Head Professional at the Wannesee Golf Club on the outskirts of Berlin. Golf was a new game in Germany and the financial opportunities were great. It was where I was born and although we returned to the UK in 1932, just as Hitler was on the rise, I continued through my school years and National Service with the RAF Regiment, which brought me to June 1951.

I found the act of hitting a golf ball very easy. This may sound arrogant but it is a statement of fact. Sadly it didn't do me much good as it might have done because I was not renowned for hours of practising and, although I won 20 tournaments which by today's standards would be considered major events, I was not able to produce my best play when the Open championship came around.

Because of the circle I was moving in, which was relatively sophisticated, I was told that I had a good turn of phrase, a quick mind and a good sense of humour. OK; so what? Suddenly out of the blue I was approached by the BBC asking if I would like to join their commentary team to give some observations as to how play was progressing. The year? 1961. I looked and marvelled at all the cables and switches and was amazed at how it all worked. They liked my style and I was asked to do several other golf events for the BBC, the largest being the Pro-Celebrity Golf series which ran for 14 years, followed by *Around with Alliss*, followed by various other spin-offs.

I have never planned for anything. That's where I've been lucky and I suppose on examination it's a gift given to very few. I don't take it for granted and am forever storing away little titbits of information in my weird and wonderful brain, and continue to enjoy the world of golf which, after all, when you examine all the facets of the game closely, is a mirror of life.

—— QUOTES ——

'If you can keep your head while all around are losing theirs, you may have misjudged the situation.'

'One good drive deserves a good second shot.'

Professor Michael Ayers, PhD

Professor of Philosophy, University of Oxford

—— FORMULA FOR SUCCESS ——

Everyone in the business knows the secret of academic success – a consuming interest in their subject, and the hard work that follows naturally from that.

Iain Banks

(also known as Iain M Banks when writing science fiction)

Writer

Persevere. Believe in yourself – but be realistic.

Success is usually about a combination of talent, luck and perseverance. You can go an amazingly long way on any one of these, but if you don't have talent you will get found out eventually, no matter how great your self belief; and if you don't have any luck you'll have to have a lot of perseverance. Conversely, if you don't persevere you're effectively trusting on your luck to win through first time.

Camila Batmanghelidjh

Director, Kids Company

I'm a psychotherapist and the founder of two children's charities. The first of these I founded when I was 25. It is called the Place 2 Be and currently offers counselling support to children in schools on a national scale. The second charity I set up when I was in my mid-thirties. It is called Kids Company and provides practical and emotional interventions for exceptionally vulnerable children, many of whom are surviving their childhoods with great courage despite horrific levels of abuse and neglect.

Kids Company was established in 1996 in order to provide practical, emotional and educational support to vulnerable inner-city children and young people. Many of the 12,000 children who come to Kids Company have experienced severe and multiple trauma. Often these are 'lone children' living in chronic deprivation, with little or no support from the adults in their family; some are young carers struggling to look after younger siblings or parents who are unable to care for them, and many have been forced into drug running, gangs, or prostitution as the only means of survival in their depleted communities.

At Kids Company we offer a safe, caring, family environment in which children's behaviour is understood in the context of their emotional pain and life experiences. We never turn a child away no matter how challenging their behaviour. Experience has taught us that children who have been exposed to violence and trauma shut down their capacities to feel in order to cope with the pain; the healing process is only possible if children's emotional resources are nurtured through consistent caring relationships.

Our aim is to promote and support emotional well-being, and in everything that we do the child is put first. We are constantly inspired by the courage and dignity expressed by vulnerable children in the face of overwhelming challenges.

Kids Company operates through two street-level centres in South London, as well as offering therapeutic and social work services in 33 schools. In 2007, Kids Company was awarded the Liberty and Justice Human Rights Award.

Don't pursue success. It never responds to being demanded. Instead, focus on delivering excellence from which success will gracefully emerge.

A short explanation of my formula … it is very important when doing a job to work at it using a deep sense of spiritual integrity. To achieve success people need positive energy. Energy will only be available if its path is not polluted, toxic or deviant. Personal ambition creates horizons limited to the self, whereas diminishing the self in the service of a greater vision and aspiration to excellence will result in achievements vaster, more complex and more embracing than one individual's capacities.

—— SUCCESS INSIGHT ——

Only in understanding how insignificant we are do we comprehend that leadership is about mobilising and being part of a greater whole. So team work, humility, preserving everyone's dignity and knowing in your heart that you are delivering quality is the gateway to success. But success is never personal, so you must never hold onto it, be seduced by it or seek definition through it. Go back to being nothing and you will be allowed to experience new successes.

—— FAVOURITE QUOTATION ——

'The virtue of the imagination is its reaching, by intuition and intensity of gaze (not reasoning, but the authoritative opening and revealing power), a more essential truth than is seen at the surface of things.' (JOHN RUSKIN)

Christopher Biggins

Actor Director, Winner of the ITV Programme 'I'm a Celebrity Get Me Out of Here' when he became 'King of the Jungle 2007'

Just be yourself. Never hide behind anyone or anything.

—— INSIGHT ——

When you're in the Jungle you have no idea what is going on in the outside world, so every morning when Ant and Dec come in to evict someone, you are convinced it's going to be you.

I always felt I would love to come fourth like David Gest did the previous year. You can imagine my surprise when I won the title King of the Jungle 2007.

The jungle was the most amazing experience of my life, I wouldn't have missed it, I loved every moment of it and I'd never do it again. Having said that I am going back at the end of the year to do a documentary on the making of it, and I can't wait.

I never saw the whole mechanism behind the show, the 600 people involved and the 70 cameras. I put my success down to just being myself. If you start acting and creating a character, you're done for. That has been my philosophy on life for ever, so it stood me in good stead for the Jungle experience. Just remember: be yourself and you will always be a winner.

—— TWO PERSONAL MANTRAS ——

'Come to terms with life very early on, this is not a dress rehearsal.'

'Go out there and enjoy every minute.'

—— QUOTE ——

'Time and tide wait for no man.'

John Bird, MBE

Founder and Editor-In-Chief of 'The Big Issue'

—— FORMULA FOR SUCCESS ——

Developing new links, getting people to work together.

All strengths are former weaknesses, otherwise they are inherent and nothing to do with you. We all have inherent strengths and weaknesses. But the ones that really matter are the strengths you make yourself, gathered and made out of what was formerly weakness.

Persevere. Hold to the course. Don't allow yourself too many distractions.

Rest well; don't boast, except to mock yourself, for you are, even in your supremacy, minuscule and insignificant beside the heroes of the past. Could you fly into the face of death as our forefathers did? Losing a contract pales into insignificance beside our ancestors' contribution.

Listen to your mistakes. They are like the trees leaves rustling in the night, reminding you of what you should have remembered.

—— QUOTE ——

I still feel deeply moved by all in *If* by Kipling:

> If you can keep your head when all about you
> Are losing theirs and blaming it on you,
> If you can trust yourself when all men doubt you
> But make allowance for their doubting too,
> If you can wait and not be tired by waiting,
> Or being lied about, don't deal in lies,
> Or being hated, don't give way to hating,
> And yet don't look too good, nor talk too wise:
> If you can dream—and not make dreams your master,
> If you can think—and not make thoughts your aim;
> If you can meet with Triumph and Disaster
> And treat those two impostors just the same;
> If you can bear to hear the truth you've spoken
> Twisted by knaves to make a trap for fools,
> Or watch the things you gave your life to, broken,
> And stoop and build 'em up with worn-out tools:
> If you can make one heap of all your winnings

And risk it all on one turn of pitch-and-toss,
And lose, and start again at your beginnings
And never breathe a word about your loss;
If you can force your heart and nerve and sinew
To serve your turn long after they are gone,
And so hold on when there is nothing in you
Except the Will which says to them: 'Hold on!'
If you can talk with crowds and keep your virtue,
Or walk with kings—nor lose the common touch,
If neither foes nor loving friends can hurt you;
If all men count with you, but none too much,
If you can fill the unforgiving minute
With sixty seconds' worth of distance run,
Yours is the Earth and everything that's in it,
And—which is more—you'll be a Man, my son!

Sir Ian Blair, QPM

Commissioner of Police of the Metropolis, London, 2005–2008

FORMULA FOR SUCCESS

No formulae can adequately address the challenges of leadership but I strive to hold four aspects of decision making pre-eminent: adequate preparation plus consistency of purpose plus flexibility as circumstances change plus, above all, understanding the need for the buy-in of others.

INSIGHTS

Let me explain that a little further. Preparation has to be the initial key to success, as that phrase '90% preparation, 10% perspiration' makes clear, but preparation is not just tactics; it includes a full understanding of the strategic intent and, of great importance, it needs to be based on the values of the organisation in question. Secondly, consistency of purpose, dedication, commitment, as in the quotation from Francis Drake, below. However, as in the competing proverbs, 'Look before you leap' and 'He who hesitates is lost', such consistency of purpose has to be balanced with the need for flexibility as the situation changes, as in the military maxim: 'No plan survives contact with the enemy'.

Above all, success in leading a team needs buy-in from the team, even those that don't agree. Two or three times I have seen brilliant people fail to understand that being right is not enough. People need to have their concerns heard, and be able, if possible, to see their contribution and viewpoint acknowledged in the plan. Merely putting someone down because you simply don't agree with their argument is not leadership.

QUOTATION

Two quotations, one from the sixteenth century and one from the twentieth:

> 'O Lord God, when Thou givest to Thy servants to endeavour any great matter, grant us also to know that it is not the beginning but the continuing of the same unto the end, which yieldeth the greater glory.' (SIR FRANCIS DRAKE)

> 'When the facts change, I change my mind. What do you do, sir?' (MAYNARD KEYNES)

Jeremy Bowen

BBC foreign correspondent. Currently BBC Middle East Editor. Has covered many of the big world stories in the last twenty years.

—— FORMULA FOR SUCCESS ——

Keep working; don't give up; make the most of the moment.

—— INSIGHTS ——

Years of covering wars has made me realise that our hold on life is fragile. That's why you have to make the most of now. Don't wait for a better time that might never come.

—— INSPIRATION ——

When I started at the BBC I admired senior colleagues like Martin Bell and Brian Barron. I also had the example of my father, Gareth Bowen, who worked for the BBC in Wales for many years.

—— INSPIRATIONAL QUOTATION ——

'Rage, rage, against the dying of the light.' (Dylan Thomas)

Jo Brand

Comedian

Success results from vigour and sacrifice.

As a fairly doting mother I can be equally inspired by one of my daughter's throwaway comments as she observes the world with wide eyed innocence as that of a line from any of the great orators, writers or thinkers – well that's just me.

However, I want to remember a 'reflection' from my old mucker and friend, Linda Smith. I can't remember what prompted the remark or the context, but she said:

> 'Rugby, what a great game for people with no fear of head injuries. And no need to fear them.'

Yes, she may have just been winding up a room full of rugger buggers and suggesting they were thick, but I rather like to speculate that she admired the union of 15 heaving hulking hunks with one aim: to get that ball over the line, come what may. Was she suggesting that personal injury, loss or cost was as nothing to the result?

It's a funny line, read into it what you wish, but there's a resonance in it for this little book.

'Don't piss down my back and then tell me it's raining.' (Spoken by Clint Eastwood in the film *The Outlaw Josey Wales*)

Gordon Brown

Prime Minister

—— FORMULA FOR SUCCESS ——

My personal formula for success is the same as my old school motto: 'I will do my utmost'. If you always give everything you have, and never stop trying, you will give yourself the best chance of success and you will never have anything to regret.

—— INSPIRATIONAL INSIGHT ——

The most inspirational story I have heard in recent years concerned the heroism of Captain David Hicks from the Royal Anglian Regiment, who led his men in a fire-fight against the Taliban in Afghanistan. He was badly wounded, but rather than retreat to safety or accept morphine, he stayed in position to lead his men through the battle, and saved many of their lives. His heroic leadership that day means that, even in death, he continues to inspire both his men and every other member of the armed forces.

—— QUOTATION ——

'Courage is the first of human qualities because it is the quality that guarantees all others.' (SIR WINSTON CHURCHILL)

Sara Campbell

World Champion Free-diver

—— JOB/CAREER ——

Free spirit – free-diver, yoga teacher, PR consultant…

—— FORMULA FOR SUCCESS ——

Find something that makes you happy, a passion, and do it to the best of your ability. And when fear whispers doubts in your ear, don't listen.

—— TIP FOR SUCCESS ——

I realised that I could be living the same life in the UK for the next 70 years! That was just unbearable and I knew I had to make a change. I'd been planning how to live a less stressful, more balanced life, but hadn't figured out how to make it work. A week's holiday in Dahab – which I never returned from! – opened my eyes to possibilities I hadn't considered before. I could hear the doubting thoughts in the back of my mind, but knew that if I gave them even the slightest attention they would grow and overwhelm the positive feelings I had about this new life. And ultimately, I had to take that leap – if it didn't work out, it would work out somewhere else. I found success by letting go of the fear that would have held me in a very unsatisfying life in London. I didn't even know what free-diving was when I moved out here, and it makes me wonder how many other people have amazing latent talents that they will never discover unless they are brave enough to step out of the 'every day' routine and do something different. I don't measure success by the world records, but by my quality of life.

—— FAVOURITE QUOTATION ——

Right to be Wrong. (JOSS STONE)

It made me realise how important it was for me to do my thing, no matter how crazy everyone else thought I was. It started with moving to Dahab in Egypt, and has taken me to World Champion Free-diver!

For me fear is the biggest barrier to success. We're afraid of failing, we're even afraid of success – more to live up to, further to fall. Where did such a level of shame at not achieving come from? Entrepreneurs understand the value of failure – it is the greatest learning experience we can have. Our fear of failure doesn't just hold us back from success, it holds us back from even trying. What a tragedy. If we don't try, we're barely living. Surely we have an obligation to make something of this amazing life we have. There are so many opportunities out there. I find it incredible – and sad – how many people say how brave I am to move to Dahab, to experiment with free-diving. As long as you're not reckless with your behaviour, you take the time to inform yourself and move ahead wisely but enthusiastically, a wonderful world awaits those who dare, although I prefer to see it not as 'daring' – simply as living.

Nick Clegg, MP

*Leader of the Liberal Democrats (since 2007), part-time lecturer at
Sheffield University and guest lecturer at Cambridge University*

—— FORMULA FOR SUCCESS ——

Success results from having the moral courage, determination and will
simply to be true to yourself.

—— INSIGHT ——

Success is often about being prepared to take risks when necessary. I am
inspired by liberals who have stuck to their principles. One of my heroes
is a North London dry cleaner, Harry Willcock. When stopped by police in
1950 and asked for his ID card he refused, with the now famous words:
'I am a Liberal. I am against that sort of thing.'

Harry was an active Liberal, having been a councillor and parliamentary
candidate. Thanks to his stand, which was supported by Liberal MPs and
Lords at the time, the ID cards programme was first challenged in the
courts and then finally scrapped. He showed that one man willing to take
a stand can change the system.

—— SUCCESS TRAITS AND INSPIRATION ——

'People care. They just don't care about politicians.'

'I hope I've inherited some of my mum's unerring compassion, her ability
to see potential in everyone, her despair at the class system, and her total
belief in justice.'

—— OTHER PERSONAL INSIGHTS ——

Favourite: music – Jonny Cash, Led Zeppelin, David Bowie, Prince, Macy
Gray, Schubert, Bach; authors – JM Coetzee, Ian McEwan, Jean Rhys;
television show – *The Office*.

Ray Clemence, MBE

Goalkeeper for Liverpool, Tottenham and England. Now National Goalkeeping Coach and Head of National teams at the Football Association

—— CAREER ——

Winner of: medals for: 5 League Championships; 3 European Cups; 2 UEFA Cups, 2 FA Cups; 1 League Cup; 7 Community Shields and 61 England Caps

—— FORMULA FOR SUCCESS ——

To listen/learn from people whom I respect with more experience than myself and always commit 100% to everything I try to achieve in my sporting life.

—— INSIGHTS ——

Never expect your sporting life to always be on a high. There are, in fact, more lows than highs. It's how you deal with both situations which make you a successful person.

When you get success, enjoy the moment, but don't get carried away within. Keep your feet on the ground, remember how you attained the successes and continue to do those things.

When you have low moments, it's how you pick yourself up to perform again. If you think about it too long, things will only get worse, learn and move on.

A personal example of that would be my being thrown out by Notts County as a 16-year-old for not being good enough, but continued to play for my local side. Three months later Scunthorpe United signed me as a professional and two years later I was signed by Liverpool FC.

Sir Terence Conran

Designer, restaurateur, retailer and writer.

It is very difficult to identify a successful formula and even harder to present a written set of rules that one may follow when plotting a route to success. I have spent a most colourful lifetime in design, in business and in retail and as you gain maturity and experience you come to understand what works and what doesn't, the things that have been successful and the things that haven't quite achieved what you set out to do. Maturity and the lessons you learn along the way are vital to success. When I was younger I was pretty selective about what I liked but I was constantly absorbing things which as I got older allowed me to see the beauty in many things.

I would advise any young designer to absorb knowledge left, right and centre. Visit design fairs, museums, exhibitions and galleries. Read books and magazines and take clippings of things of things you like; use a digital camera to record things that inspire you and feed your imagination with ideas; create a scrap book in your mind that you can always draw from. Talk to designers and artists; gain practical experience and learn a craft so you understand how things are actually made and how different materials shape the design process. I have always concerned myself with what one may call the practical aspects of design and tried to relate my work to the manufacturing process. I have never designed any product that I wouldn't know how to make myself.

In the simplest terms, I could perhaps attribute most of my success to having a keen and discerning eye – a visual certainty a strong conviction in my instincts. I can see something and say immediately 'that's good', 'that will work' or 'that will sell', but best of all: 'that's really beautiful'. I have had many incredible role models and mentors down the years and have received many pearls of wisdom but nothing has proved to be quite so emphatically true as 'if at first you don't succeed, try, try and try again'. I suppose this has given me a tenacity and a belief in my work that has always served me well.

I have learned that some of the most important qualities to succeed are intelligence, imagination, creativity, common sense, perseverance, market awareness, determination, sensitivity and above all, a thick skin of self confidence. Perhaps these values appear to cancel each other out, but I believe they are all necessary attributes required for different times and in different situations.

And although it is perhaps the most appealing quality, frustration has led me in to many ventures that have ultimately proved successful, not least with Habitat. After leaving the Central School I was young, hungry and perhaps a little naïve. I spent the next decade trying to get my designs in the public eye but found it an infuriating process. By the early sixties I had had a modicum of success selling contract furniture to commercial users but I had a fierce conviction that there was a great opportunity for me to sell my furniture to a wider domestic audience – which is what I had set out to achieve. And so began my Habitat experiment.

—— TIPS FOR SUCCESS ——

Another important lesson I have absorbed over the years is that design and business are completely interlinked – one cannot succeed without the other. I've always thought that design was 98% common sense and 2% aesthetics. It is the same with business except the magic ingredient is vision. More than ever now – as the Chairman of a company working on hundreds of projects around the world – I have come to realise that positive leadership conveys a clear message and vision to your staff and is vital. Enthusing your staff with passion and dedication to your business goes a long way to achieving success.

Perhaps I am lucky in that everything I have done for work or for business I would do for pleasure. Always enjoy what you do; have fun. Don't be afraid of making mistakes because I would wager that every single one of the illustrious contributors to this book has at some point in their career made a mistake. Learn from them, adapt to bad situations and emerge on the other side wiser and better equipped for the experience. Because if you believe in yourself, and if you believe in your ideas then you must never give up. Perhaps that is as close as I could ever come to defining success.

Sir Henry Cooper, OBE, KSG

Former heavyweight boxer. British, European and Commonwealth Heavyweight champion in 1970. The only British boxer to win three Lonsdale Belts outright.

—— FORMULA FOR SUCCESS (IN THE RING) ——

'When in doubt, stick your left out.' This got me out of a lot of trouble.

Sir Robert Crawford, CBE

Former Director-General, Imperial War Museum

Success is only as good as tomorrow's performance and is for others to judge. I have no personal formula but the advice I have learned from others, which I have endeavoured to follow, is to be oneself, work hard, master the detail of business, make and keep friends, set clear objectives, gather talented and trustworthy people around you (especially one's boss), heed their advice, encourage, empower and enable them to achieve collective goals, confess and forgive mistakes, and recognise and reward achievements.

I have been fortunate to work for a number of distinguished airmen. The first, to whom I am indebted for my first job, and consequently my career, for all my professional training and for a succession of unique opportunities to develop management experience taught his staff 'to start as you mean to go on', that 'knowledge is power' and that 'the ideal is the enemy of the good'. Delegation I learned from him and my father (not a military person), who was especially fond of the maxim, 'Don't keep a dog and bark yourself' but equally taught his children to face up to the tough decisions and 'never to take the line of least resistance'. The virtue of decisiveness (which I do not claim to possess), I was taught by our then Chairman, a former Battle of Britain squadron commander who rose to the highest rank. Following a particularly tricky meeting at which he had brought discussion of a complex and worrying matter to a decisive conclusion, I remarked that he had a rare facility for resolving issues in clear black and white terms. He gently reminded me that when you have an Me 109 in your mirror or your sights, you have no option but to act decisively if you wish to survive.

I think the poem must be Kipling's 'If', partly because of his place in the story of the Great War, the ninetieth anniversary of whose ending we mark this year, and partly because a framed copy of it was presented to me at an impressionable age. The opening line is salutary warning to Chief Executives of Non-Departmental Public Bodies.

Peter Cullum, PHD, MSC, FCII, ACIM

UK Insurance Market Entrepreneur, 'Management Today'
2008 Entrepreneur of the Year

Traditionally trained manager in both UK- and US-owned insurance companies reaching board and managing director level at the age of 38. MSc at age 24. Headhunted to lead a small regional insurance company in some difficulty in 1992. A significant turnaround followed by a successful management buyout led to reappraisal of current market models and ultimately the creation (as principal shareholder) of a M&A specialist and consolidator in the UK insurance market – 10 years later the largest privately-owned insurance intermediary in Europe having acquired and successfully integrated 142 insurance businesses. Marketing still the first love. Ernst & Young UK Entrepreneur of the Year 2006, Private Company of the Year 2007, 2007 UK Management Team of the Year.

—— FORMULA FOR SUCCESS ——

'Knowing is useless without doing'.

—— EXPLANATION OF FORMULA ——

Plenty of people know all the answers, but few bother to put the answers into practice. It is the action-orientated who win, not the know-alls.

People make the difference, enjoy enthusing and motivating them. Business is not a game of pure logic! It is emotional, exciting and occasionally scary!

—— TIPS FOR SUCCESS ——

Never, ever assume the person you are dealing with, selling to etc, is smarter than you. Even if they prove that they are very smart, that does not mean they are as committed as you, nor do they have the team you have. Lead by example, plan everything in advance. Keep yourself fit and have a desire to never stop learning.

Passion, and the energy to put that passion to work are key, but one individual can never do the job alone. Others must share the passion or be led to that passion. Find good people who can share the dream and don't let them go.

Never accept that where you are is satisfactory. Reinvent the business every 3 years, at least.

Edward de Bono, MA, MD, PhD, DPhil, LLD

Thinker

If I had to put together a formula for success it would be as follows: Courage, clear thinking and not minding what others say.

While there as many as 50,000 people worldwide writing software for computers, we have made no effort at all to write software for the human brain for 2,400 years. We have been very satisfied and complacent with the software developed by the GG3 (the Greek Gang of three). The thinking developed by Aristotle, Plato and Socrates is excellent just as the rear left wheel of a motor car is excellent – but it is not enough.

When Greek thinking came into Europe at the time of the Renaissance, schools, universities and thinking in general were in the hands of the Church. They had no need for design thinking. What the Church needed was truth, logic and argument with which to prove heretics wrong. So we have a judgement-based thinking which has been excellent in technical matters and very inadequate in human affairs.

Creative thinking has always been regarded as a mystery or magic talent given only to some. From my research work on the more complicated systems of the human body, I worked out some principles of self-organising systems. I applied these to the behaviour of the human brain in the book *The Mechanism of Mind* (1969). This book was very well received by the leading physicist in the world who received his Nobel Prize for discovering the quark (Professor Murray Gell-Mann). He commissioned a team of computer experts to simulate what I said in the book and they confirmed that the system worked exactly as I had predicted.

From this basis I designed the formal tolls of lateral thinking which turn idea creativity into a skill instead of a magic talent. There are also perceptual tools taught in thousands of schools worldwide and mandatory in some countries. Then there is the Six Hat method of parallel thinking which is much more constructive and much quicker than traditional argument. All these methods are now widely in use around the world.

All the time there has been considerable opposition from journalists and others. This is motivated by jealousy fuelled by ignorance of what I am talking about. It is necessary to go your own way and not to be deterred by the opinions of others. They are nearly always negative with regard to anything really new – as Einstein said in his day.

When I proposed to write a book with the title 'Why I want to be king of Australia', most of my acquaintances did not like the idea at all. They thought it pretentious and presumptuous. So I wrote the book which was well received (given the Australian sense of humour). I even discussed with the prime minister having a new referendum with three choices: Queen of England; Republic; or de Bono for King.

One education critic once said that some of the methods were so simple they could not work. But they do work and research by Atkey showed that teaching the methods as a separate subject improved performance in every other subject by between 30 and 100%.

So do not be afraid to do your own thing even if others (through ignorance and jealousy) do not approve.

—— QUOTATION ——

'You can analyse the past but you have to design the future.' (EDWARD DE BONO)

Peter Duncan

Chief Scout, actor, former presenter of the BBC TV programme 'Blue Peter'

—— INSIGHTS ——

When I was a little boy I would dream that I would find a Superman costume at the end of my bed so I would be allowed to use my super powers secretly for the benefit of others.

When I think back over my life the two roles I have undertaken which have in some way contributed to that ideal is as a Blue Peter presenter and as Chief Scout No. 9. Over the last 50 years, Blue Peter has encouraged children to look beyond themselves at the wonder of the world around them and to contribute by action in helping charitable causes both at home and abroad. The world scouting movement applies a similar ethos in that a good action towards another benefits not only the well being of the receiver but a sense of achievement in the giver.

I have simply been a front man, the messenger, using what communication skills I have to promote good ideas. I have tried to embody the spirit as opposed to the form of these two institutions and if I did have a formula for success, it would be not to allow an overcomplicated system of rules, regulations and habit to detract from an instinctive approach to life.

—— INSPIRATIONAL QUOTATION ——

As an actor I try not to get too carried away with good reviews, so to add a little Ying to the Yang, here is Shakespeare's Macbeth to bring some perspective.

> Life's but a walking shadow: a poor player,
> That struts and frets his hour upon the stage
> And then is heard no more: it is a tale
> Told by an idiot, full of sound and fury
> Signifying nothing.

Dawn Dyne

Marie Curie Cancer Care's Nursing Ambassador for England

CAREER

Marie Curie Nurses provide free end of life care to people with a terminal illness, giving them the choice to spend their last days at home supported by their loved ones. I became a Marie Curie Nurse because I feel very strongly that everyone deserves dignity and respect at the end of their lives. As an ambassador for the charity I attend fundraising and media events around the country to help raise awareness of the work of the Marie Curie Nursing Service.

FORMULA FOR SUCCESS

My motto is 'Live in the day' which I try and get my patients to adopt.

INSIGHT

I remember one man I was looking after had me searching through cupboards to find photos and memorabilia of his life. Eventually we sat down and started looking through everything and before long, we were both laughing. As the night progressed we made so much noise that we woke up his wife! The next morning when I left, the couple were looking through the photo albums together and I felt glad I'd set that in motion. It meant they could reflect on their life and talk about their memories.

When I laugh with my patients, I know their laughter comes from the heart. They're so ill, so it's not superficial happiness and they're not putting up a front; it is true laughter.

INSPIRATION

What inspires me most about my work is the patients and families I am so privileged to care for. As a Marie Curie Nurse, I work closely with the family, listening to their worries and concerns and helping to prepare them for what lies ahead. People say it must be a very upsetting job, but I don't find it upsetting at all. It is very rewarding when you can help a family who are both emotionally and physically drained and patients who are struggling psychologically, to help them make decisions. When all the issues have been dealt with, it is lovely to see them at peace. This is what

I feel makes Marie Curie Nurses so special. I have received many thank you cards from the families of patients I have cared for. This is an extract from one of the cards:

> 'Thank you for being with us and with mum on the night she died. It was such a comfort to know that she was in such good hands. I can't begin to know how you cope with such situations all the time but I thank the Lord that there are people like you who can. It made such a difference to us all at a very difficult time.'

Witnessing the love between family members and being there for them is an honour. So is seeing the smiles on the faces of patients when I arrive and the relief on the faces of their families who know that I am there to care for their loved one while they get some rest.

On my way to work in the car I often say these few words from a hymn by Frances Ridley Havergal to prepare me for the situation I am going into.

O give thine own sweet rest to me
That I may speak with soothing power
A word in season as from thee
To weary ones in needful hour

Bernie Ecclestone

President and CEO of Formula One Management and Formula One Administration. Co-owner of Queens Park Rangers Football Club.

—— EARLY CAREER HIGHLIGHTS ——

I left school at 16 to work and to pursue my motorcycle hobby; then I did a BSc in chemical engineering at Woolwich Polytechnic. After the Second World War, I traded spare motorcycle parts and then later co-founded Compton and Ecclestone. I entered 500cc formula junior series with some modest success but gave this up in 1951 to focus on a business career. Following a period managing Weekend Car Auction, in 1957 I managed Stuart Lewis-Evans and purchased F1 Connaught racing team. I became manager of Jochen Rindt and partial owner of Lotus. In '72, I purchased the Brabham racing team and then formed Formula 1 Constructor's Association.

Many people say that I have been instrumental in developing Formula 1 into a highly professional commercially successful sport. That is for others to judge. What I am personally most proud of is the part I have played in improving safety technology. We have done more for safety than anything else. Nowadays, drivers can get out of their cars practically unharmed, even after the most apparently horrendous accidents.

—— FORMULA FOR SUCCESS ——

Luck, experience and stamina (principally).

I don't really know the secret of my success. Nor will the chef of an exclusive restaurant with three Michelin stars be able to tell you, because success doesn't depend on a single, secret ingredient. It's the sum of many details and activities. I could add further success factors which are a product of experience. I have been in the business a long time; that means I am trusted and respected.

—— INSIGHT ——

My insight, as someone who is 12 years above the official retirement age, relates to ageism and is therefore, perhaps, most relevant to the older readers of this book – say 50 plus – although, having said that, it might be useful to their families to understand that the brain does not go into stand-by function on the 65th anniversary of their birth.

In 1999, I had a triple coronary bypass operation and I was urged to retire. What for? People retire to die, don't they? They think 'I've come to the end of my useful life and the next thing I have to do is die'. So they wait. My view is that age has nothing to do with it. There's plenty of very active, good people that are dumped by companies when they are 65. Yet they keep people who are 40 who are useless.

I am fortunate in that I like what I do, so why should I stop? I won't even think about it. My wife says they'll probably have to carry my dead body off the track. Or bury me in the tour bus. This stems simply from an attitude of mind that I would argue is relevant to everyone who enjoys work and wants to keep mentally active. They just need, like me, to really want to do it.

That is not to say that I think I am irreplaceable – nobody is. Death is rather inevitable, and there is nothing you can do about it. Formula 1 is properly established now and will probably do as well or better without me.

There are some positive aspects of getting old. Imagine now that I did something quite evil and the judge said to me 'Life imprisonment!' – it wouldn't worry me very much. But if I was 21, I'd be super upset!!

—— TIP FOR SUCCESS ——

First rule of business is never to let your rivals know what you are thinking, let alone what you are about to do next.

—— INSPIRATIONAL QUOTATIONS ——

'Some men succeed by what they know; some by what they do, and a few by what they are.' (ELBERT HUBBARD)

'Success is not the key to happiness. Happiness is the key to success. If you love what you are doing, you will be successful.' (ALBERT SCHWEITZER)

Ranulph Fiennes

Expedition Leader and Travel Writer

'When taking over a new job, make sure your predecessor tells you all the costly lessons that he or she learned.'

My main tips for success are, as above, on the negative side. So my other tip for success is more of a positive nature. It is: 'Don't be put off by all the apparent obstacles. The very act of starting the ball rolling will shift quite a few of them.'

'Always a little further pilgrim, beyond the next …'

There is never any point crying over spilt milk because, in order to win at some of your big goals, you are bound to lose at others along the way.

Lord Foster of Thames Bank, OM

Architect

Norman Foster is the Chairman and Founder of the global practice Foster and Partners. He studied at Manchester University School of Architecture and Yale University, where he gained a Masters Degree. In 1967, he established Foster Associates (now Foster + Partners) which has grown to become a uniquely respected company bridging architecture, infrastructure, city planning and product design. He was awarded the Pritzker Architecture Prize in 1999, and the Praemium Imperiale in 2002. He was granted a Knighthood in1990 and appointed to the Order of Merit in 1997. In 1999, he became a life peer, taking the title Lord Foster of Thames Bank.

—— FORMULA FOR SUCCESS ——

'Think global: act local.'

—— INSIGHTS ——

As an architect you are only as powerful as your advocacy. While you may have a profound understanding of issues such as global warming and the search for sustainable solutions, you have to acknowledge that this can only be applied project by project. Some clients are open to sustainable solutions; others less so. Yet even small steps in the right direction are better than none at all.

I grew up in a working-class neighbourhood of Manchester. I saw how my father's health suffered from over-work in the Metrovick factory and I have my own student memories of appalling conditions in industry at the time as I worked to pay my way through university. The anger that grew in me then drove me as an architect to improve the conditions of ordinary people through building – whether that was in the factory, the office or the public realm. It reinforced a fundamental belief that architecture is rooted in the needs of people – material and spiritual, measurable and intangible.

—— INSPIRATIONAL QUOTATION ——

'We shape our buildings; thereafter they shape us.' (WINSTON CHURCHILL)

Architecture must have the ability to transcend function, to add beauty as well as value; to lift the spirits, to move us in some way. When I first entered the architectural profession there was an accepted demarcation between 'architecture' – a high art – and what was regarded as mere 'building'. I have always rejected such distinctions. Design for me is all-encompassing. It is about values. I believe one has a moral duty to design well and to design responsibly – whether that is at the scale of a door handle or a city masterplan. To design is to question and to challenge. Design can explore the new and build on the past. It can transform patterns of health, living and working. It is not only individual buildings but also the wider context that affects our well being. Design can be a catalyst in improving the environment, especially in cities. Holistic thinking can be applied to infrastructure – transport systems, bridges, stations, streets and public spaces – the 'urban glue' that holds cities together, just as it is to buildings. Above all design is a human act. While the means may be technical, the goals are social.

Sir Roger Gibbs

*Former Chairman of Gerrard and National plc, The London Discount Market,
The Wellcome Trust, St Paul's Cathedral Foundation,
Fleming Family and Partners*

Centenary President of the Cresta Run, Commentator on America's ABC 'Wide World of Sport,' Ran in the 1982 London Marathon (beat 2042, beaten by 14,307), 3 'O' Levels – 4 Honorary Doctorates.

—— FORMULA FOR SUCCESS ——

My formula for success in life of course includes hard work but there are other vital elements. Be a good listener, always put yourself in the place of those to whom you are talking, be enthusiastic, be single-mindedly determined, never give in and be extraordinarily lucky! This combination will give you every chance of being successful but will also provide you with the ammunition to inspire others.

—— INSIGHTS ——

I am certain that success in life should not, indeed cannot, be measured in monetary terms. However, it is important that any financial success should, at least in part, be used as an influence for good, whether it be through charitable giving, the gainful employment of others or helping individuals much less fortunate that oneself.

I approach the question of success from the point of view of the schoolboy struggler and late developer – because I was both. It has always given me the greatest pleasure to see so many who didn't make much of an impression at school, flourish so spectacularly in later life. I don't just mean Sir Winston Churchill but countless others from every generation. This fact seems to come as a surprise to most, but it shouldn't – it's obvious.

As we all know, children grow up at different speeds and at different stages. The education system doesn't help the schoolboy or schoolgirl struggler or late developer as much as it should. It doesn't take these children's particular situations into account. Perhaps it is unfair to ask it to do so – but how I wish it would. The slow starters have no alternative but to try and develop a certain native cunning and become somewhat streetwise to survive at school at all. From an early age they already know instinctively that life is tough and that the world will never owe them a living. Many of these are well prepared for the rigours of the outside world. Of course, the talented and dedicated high flyers are better prepared than any but never underestimate some of those who are sluggish out of the gate.

It is clearly a great advantage to be a good communicator but the most precious quality of all, I believe, is enthusiasm – preferably controlled enthusiasm. It is so much easier to quieten unbridled enthusiasm than to inspire someone who doesn't want to be inspired.

One thing you always need in life is luck. As a director of Arsenal Football Club, I always thought that the players were incredibly fortunate to be under Arsene Wenger. He is the ultimate, thoughtful, caring and hugely effective motivator. An example of his influence is Ray Parlour who, until Wenger's arrival, was a squad player of no particular merit. In just two years Arsene Wenger instilled into Parlour belief in himself and his own ability. Ray Parlour responded so positively that he became a highly rated player and a vital part of the hugely successful Arsenal team of 2003–2004. Arsene Wenger is a magical football manager but Ray Parlour was incredibly lucky to meet him.

I was also very lucky in who I met along the way. So many helped me. After a free transfer from Eton, when I was told they'couldn't do anything more for me'I went to Millfield. Despite years of encouragement from my wonderful parents, my four brothers and my sister, I didn't seem to make any progress at almost anything – but I was determined not to end up as the runt of the litter. However, the turning point for me was almost certainly when at Millfield I was taught English Language by the playwright to be, Robert Bolt, who wrote 'A Man for All Seasons'. Bolt turned those lucky enough to be his pupils into believing in themselves and to be much more effective at expressing themselves. We all owe Robert Bolt so much – but no one more than I.

Duncan Goose

Founder and Managing Director of Global Ethics Limited.
Winner of ITV's Great Britons Award in 2007 in the Campaigner category.
Winner of a Beacon Fellowship Trust Award and recipient of the Paul Harris
Fellowship Award presented by Rotary International.

—— FORMULA FOR SUCCESS ——

You have nothing to lose, and everything to win by taking chances. If you accept that the worst thing that could happen is death, then everything else is a bonus.

—— INSIGHTS ——

My parents and grandparents were my biggest sources of inspiration.

From a young age my parents encouraged me to work. Starting at the age of 10, I held a different job each year – paperboy, butcher's assistant, decorator, farm labourer, floor sweeper and salesman. Late teens saw me being a beach barman and marketing assistant. If nothing else, it gave me great insights into the value of a good team and how to transcend social hierarchy.

My grandparents also played a key role in formative years. My grandfather had always fought for people's rights in his role as a civic counsellor, even into his early 80s, and my grandmother was a huge champion for Dr Barnado's and other charitable projects. I was encouraged to participate wherever possible.

By my early 20s, during the recession, I joined a start-up marketing agency. The founders were a team of enthusiastic and determined people who honed my beliefs into the work-hard, play-hard ethic, which was always underpinned with treating people with respect and support.

In 1998, I took a leave of absence and rode a motorbike around the world. That odyssey taught me a great deal, and to value life. Along that journey I'd had a nasty accident in Canada which almost cost me my eyesight; I'd been shot at in Mexico; caught in a hurricane which killed 30,000 people in Honduras; I'd survived an earthquake in Indonesia and been rescued by the police in Baluchistan – somewhere I shouldn't have been without a military escort. Despite all this, it was the warmth, humility and generosity of people all over the world that touched me the most.

My return in to the world of commerce was relatively simple and whilst working for WPP was great fun and a challenge, it didn't quite feel like the big challenge I was now looking for.

Global Ethics was born out of a desire to effect change in the world. The founding principles of the company were to generate maximum profits, but then to give it away to charitable causes.

To run a start-up business is a challenge in itself, but to run one without start-up capital and no residual profits? People thought I was mad. Some of them were the same doubters who said I'd never ride a motorbike around the world.

In its first full year of trading, Global Ethics donated £835,000.

In order to achieve this, Global Ethics launched a brand of bottled spring water, called One. All the profits from One water fund amazing roundabout powered water pumps called Playpumps. We install these in schools in Africa and as children play, a free, clean water supply is pumped from deep underground into storage tanks for the community. Not only does the community benefit from the water supply, but it means that children now attend school rather than walk for hours a day to collect water. Water for water. Simple.

Our initial goal was to try and change one life. We now change hundreds of thousands a year.

—— TIPS FOR SUCCESS ——

Simply, to aim as high and as far away as you can possibly imagine and work as hard as you possibly can towards it. The bigger the challenge the better, but don't be afraid to look back to see how far you've come and celebrate the successes, however small they are.

—— INSPIRATIONAL QUOTATION ——

'It is hard to fail, but it is worse never to have tried to succeed.'

(THEODORE ROOSEVELT, 26th President of the United States of America.
Inscribed on the wall of the American Museum
of Natural History, New York City)

Wing Commander Andrew D Green, OBE, MA, RAF

*Fighter pilot, Royal Air Force; Captain, Royal Air Force Cresta Team;
Holder, World Land Speed Record*

'Because we can!'

Actually, this is more completely expressed as 'Possunt quia posse videntur'. It is the motto of my first squadron, No. 19 (Fighter) Squadron, flying the mighty Phantom when I was there. It means 'They can because they think they can' – and trust me, whenever the opportunity arose and whatever the activity, we did!

Of course, it means two different things, depending on how you read it. It can be taken as an inspiringly positive (if slightly twee) statement of the power of positive thought. Or it can be used as an excuse for fighter pilots to spend their whole lives behaving like 12-year-olds, seeing what they can get away with and doing things just for fun … just 'because they can'.

—— INSPIRATION/TIP FOR SUCCESS ——

Sometimes you need to ignore how really difficult something is, and just do it. The most extraordinary proponent of this has to be Richard Noble. I have never met anyone who can look down the wrong end of a telescope and declare 'Look, that problem is tiny and it's miles away' with such conviction that you believe him, even though you know what he's doing. And even though he's talking about the elephant that's actually in the room with you at the time.

Sometimes this is the only way to move forward, and it's occasionally a wonderful thing (in a slightly terrifying kind of way) to experience. I suspect that I was predisposed to appreciate it though, as I appear to have been doing it for some time.

At school, I ignored all of the (very real and well presented) obstacles that my family raised to me being a fighter pilot. Once at college, I ignored the difficulties of having almost no previous experience, and being far too skinny, in getting into one of the Oxford University rowing squads. In considering the Royal Air Force as a career, I did not even realise, let alone consider, the fact that I was by no means a natural pilot. I would have to work very hard, every day, at flying jet fighters if I was to have any chance of doing the job. On the Cresta Run, on the other hand, I was very painfully aware that I was just about the worst beginner that the Royal Air Force had ever tried to train on the Cresta – but, for reasons that I still can't explain, I kept going back anyway. Somehow, to my continued amazement, I am now their No. 1 rider and Captain of the Royal Air Force Team. Looking back at this list, I wonder if I could have made more sensible choices and found something easier to do – but I wouldn't change any of them. Being a Fighter Pilot, rowing for Oxford, riding the Cresta Run have all been amazing experiences and have all been life-changing in some way. And then there's Richard Noble …

When I first read that this eccentric Englishman was planning to build a supersonic car (and being a pilot, I had an inkling of just how hard that would be), I thought he was completely barking. Thirteen years and two land speed records later – 763 mph for the unlimited World Land Speed Record, and 350 mph for the world's fastest diesel car – I know that I was right. Completely barking. At this point I have to pause and ask myself, so what does that make me? Richard, in the meantime, has not slowed down for a second. We were discussing an idea for a new (and fairly huge) project recently, in which he felt sure that the Ministry of Defence could take a key role. I tried to explain that it wasn't that simple, and that use of government assets would require the approval of someone very important – it's the sort of thing that the Prime Minster would get to hear about. His response? 'Right, we'll go and see the Prime Minster then.' Not much you can say to that. Just ignore how difficult it is, and do it anyway …

—— INSPIRATIONAL QUOTATION ——

'A ship in port is safe, but that is not what ships are for. Sail out to sea and do new things.' (Rear Admiral Grace Murray Brewster Hopper, USN)

—— A LAST THOUGHT ——

My other inspiration is a girl called Emma. One of the leading authorities in her field (she's an eye specialist), she's clever, modest to a fault, endlessly cheerful, generous, warm, kind, funny and gorgeous to look at. Of course, as soon as I realised all of this (which did not take long), I married her.

Zyg Gregorek, BA Econ (Hons)

Partner/Director of Fish Farming business; Entrepreneur; World's greatest fisherman; awarded the 'Shark Royal Slam', the 'Billfish Royal Slam' and the 'Tuna Royal Slam' by the International Game Fish Association.

—— FORMULA FOR SUCCESS ——

Change the 'no' to 'go' or 'yes'.

—— CAREER ——

I am a very happily married man (32 years in 2008) to a wonderful wife, Rose, and 3 lovely daughters. I have, with the help of my wife created from scratch, many successful businesses. Anglers Paradise started with one lake and five villas in 1985 on 35 acres; we have now become the biggest of our type in the world: 37 villas, swimming pool, play area, African safari bar and Fisherman's bar, BBQ area etc. Over 30 lakes, all built from scratch, set in stunning countryside of over 170 acres. This includes Golden Lake Fisheries, Anglers Eldorado, Anglers Shangri La and Anglers Nirvana.

—— INSIGHTS ——

I can claim up to 10 nationalities but I am proud to have a British passport and fly the flag of St George whenever I go fishing around the world. English is my third language. Polish was first, then Swahili and when I first went to school I could not speak a word of English. My earliest memories were living as a refugee in East Africa (Kenya, Uganda and Tanganyika) in mud huts with no running water or electricity. My family were very well connected in Poland, big estates and even a Cardinal in Rome (Cardinal Slepy). My grandparents lost everything including most of my uncles who were killed in the Katyn massacres.

After terrible suffering and deprivation in Siberia, we ended up in East Africa. I was born on the way in Karachi, which was then India but is now Pakistan. Although material things were missing, I had the most important things: love and affection from my grandparents and my mother. When I first went to kindergarten in the camp, I used to run away; in the end they took me to kindergarten the other side of camp, locked me in the classroom for half an hour. When I was let out I ran away again and they could not catch me and I got back before my grandparents. Discipline was strict and I remember many times being punished by being made to kneel on dried peas.

My mother became a teacher and then a hotel manageress so I spent most of my time in the beginning with my grandparents. I had a crocodile as pet, monkeys, bush babies, dogs, parrots etc. My grandparents and mother were great entrepreneurs. My mother left the camp and my grandparents opened a shop or a small stall. My grandmother used to bake bread and make salami, buy pigs from the natives and slaughter them at home. Grandad was a bit naughty and would distil vodka and sell it; the police raided us many times, but they never found anything. I remember once when they came I had to lie on the bed crying and sobbing, pretending to be very ill as the vodka was under the bed. Another time when they went to a Masai village to buy meat, a Masai grabbed me, threw his cloak around me and started running off; I pulled his plonker, he yelled and dropped me. Another lucky escape was running on the branches over an open latrine, falling in and passing out; it took a few days in hospital to recover (almost as bad as when I had tapeworm which was also unpleasant). Other scrapes would be some of the following: I remember visiting somebody who had a lion in an enclosure. As I was small and skinny I managed to get through the fence and threw stones at it; everybody started yelling at me; I thought they were applauding me and continued. Fortunately the lion was not hungry and ignored me, so I got bored and came out, upon which I was grabbed and spanked. Another time I threw coconuts at a hippo that chased me; luckily he gave up the chase. When I tried to catch my first fish, I chased a mudskipper and got stuck in quicksand; there was a bush nearby and I managed to get out. On the same beach I escaped the swing of a giant stingray, which native fishermen had caught. I had gone to examine it and prodded it with a stick. I went to five different primary schools before ending up in the Commonwealth Grammar School.

—— INSPIRATIONAL QUOTATION ——

'Nothing happens until you make it happen.'

Dame Tanni Grey-Thompson, DBE

Speaker, presenter, paralympian

'Aim high even if you hit a cabbage.'

This phrase was often used by my grandfather, and means that you should always have a goal or a dream to aim for, and even if you don't always reach your goal at least you have tried, because if you don't try you never know what you can do.

—— INSIGHT ——

In the 1980s, I watched a documentary on two Welsh athletes: Chris Hallam and John Harris. It was inspirational stuff and both men inspired me in different ways.

John was asked what he would most like to do and when he said 'have a heart attack running for a bus', I thought it was a brilliant way to handle being in a wheelchair. There was no self-pity, just a gentle self-mockery in his attitude. Chris on the other hand shook up disability sport with his bleached-blonde hair and tiger-print racing suits. When I saw Chris compete in the London Marathon in 1985, I thought: I'd like to race London; I want to be an athlete.

Guy Hands

Financier and investor

—— CAREER ——

(this piece of text written for, but provided by, Mr Hands)

Guy Hands is a man who has gone his own way, often against all odds, to build a remarkable business empire. His story shows how self-belief can yield extraordinary results.

Born in 1959, he grew up in an ordinary family in Kent. State educated, he overcame serious dyslexia to make it to Oxford. Anecdotes from his early life show an individual streak: he nearly blew up a school laboratory and once played Lady Macbeth in a school play.

Starting work in the City in 1982 – as a bond trader on the Goldman Sachs floor – he felt himself to be something of an outsider in the 'old school tie' environment. It was not long, however, before he found his own way of breaking new ground: post the 1989 credit crash, he set up the Goldman Asset Structuring Group which used securitisation and other creative techniques to generate income streams from illiquid assets and businesses.

In 1994, he proposed starting a principal finance business at Goldman Sachs, where Goldman would use its own money to buy businesses. Goldman Sachs rejected getting into the business. He therefore looked for other backers, joining Nomura in December 1994 to set up Nomura Principal Finance, the first business of its kind in the City, later to be imitated by most major banks.

Buying unpopular businesses on Nomura's behalf, he invariably sold them at a profit. His instinct for the right investments, including chains of UK pubs, betting chain William Hill – and Angel Trains, a rolling stock company, netted profits of around £2.75bn.

In 2002, he set up his own business, Terra Firma, where he has invested around €7,089m to buy unloved companies, with spectacular results. His latest challenge was to buy troubled music business EMI, which he is now restructuring.

'I did it my way.'

In business, and in life, you will never succeed unless you have the courage of your convictions. Being successful in business means leadership, having a vision and sticking to it, even when everyone else thinks you are wrong.

── TIP FOR SUCCESS ──

Make the most of your weaknesses, as well as your strengths. Your weaknesses are what make you different. There are a lot of good bankers. But if you're the one with a difficulty of some kind, and you find a way round it, that may well make you that bit more creative– and be the basis for your success.

Some commentators have said that my early dyslexia made me analyse business information in a different, more practical way, because I couldn't read through long documents, and perhaps that is true. Turn your weaknesses to your own advantage.

── INSPIRATIONAL POEM ──

I am known to be more of a karaoke than a poetry man. However, being a contrarian investor, I am going instead for a contrarian choice of poem. Kipling is unfashionable today but his much-quoted poem, *If*, does capture the spirit of what we do in Terra Firma, and how I have always tried to be in life.

> **IF** you can keep your head when all about you
> Are losing theirs and blaming it on you,
> If you can trust yourself when all men doubt you …'
> As an investor, I'd also have to draw attention to these lines:
> 'If you can make one heap of all your winnings
> And risk it on one turn of pitch-and-toss,
> And lose, and start again at your beginnings
> And never breathe a word about your loss…'

── FINAL INSIGHT ──

Overall, being able to form my own opinions and fight for them has been essential to my success.

Judie (Devlin) Hashman

Badminton player

—— CAREER SUMMARY ——

In my era, before badminton was included in the Olympic or Commonwealth Games, there was only one 'Grand Slam' tournament for badminton players – a veritable 'Wimbledon' and 'World Championships' rolled into one, called the All-England Championships. It was the only occasion (in the years when propeller planes took 24 hours to cross the Atlantic and an overnight stopover to arrive from Asia) that all the world's top players gathered at the same venue. My record was to win ten All-England women's singles titles (still unequalled) and seven All-England women's doubles titles between 1954 and 1967.

During my career, I won over 80 national and international titles including the 'Open' championships of Scotland, Ireland, USA, Canada, Jamaica, India, Singapore, Germany, Holland and Sweden and a European Championships Gold Medal.

I was unbeaten in singles, anywhere in the world, for five years between 1960 and 1964 (inclusive) and am the only badminton player to be included in the International Women's Sports Hall of Fame.

—— FORMULA FOR SUCCESS ——

Success comes from performing a simple task with consistency and at a high standard on a regular basis. With good quality and concentrated repetition comes excellence. Being 'flashy' and 'exotic' are no routes to sustained success.

—— INSIGHT ——

In a word, practise. Some people hate it, but I loved it and it is essential to achieve sporting success. I pitted my wits against the shuttle, the net and the lines on the far side of the court. It was a love-love affair. I loved practising and I loved trying to create the perfect shot. In over 30 years of playing badminton, I believe I created the 'perfect' game just twice. When I did, it was the realisation of a dream and the world stood still. Sounds and sights were distorted. I was in another place, outside myself, yet physically on court – an experience which was (and still is!) indescribable and never-to-be-forgotten.

—— TIPS FOR SUCCESS ——

It is imperative to understand and acknowledge any of your own weaknesses and then address them before your opponents discover them. In order to remain at the top for a long succession of years, you must be vigilant, observant, self-critical, agreeable to change/alteration and open-minded.

You need to know yourself better than others know you. And you need to watch others perform so that you are not surprised by what they produce, so that you can consider incorporating their best assets into your own repertoire and so that you can identify their weaknesses.

Although a reputation might mean something for my opponents to worry about (and thus gain me a psychological advantage), I knew that I was only as good as my most recent result. I reviewed my results annually to put the year into perspective and to work out where improvements and adjustments needed to be made.

I found it easy to look at my accomplishments negatively because I was always aware that, to remain at the top, it was necessary to constantly discover areas for improvement.

—— INSPIRATIONAL QUOTATION ——

At a very early age, my father (himself a multiple winner of the All-England Championships), who was a stickler for good footwork and correct stroke production, said to me in a serious voice but with a small twinkle in his eye:

> 'Don't ever let me see an action photo of you with incorrect footwork.'

I never forgot this.

Honed stroke production and correct footwork not only gave me more choices but, more importantly, created a priceless gift: deception. Deception then gave me time. Time gave me control. If you are in control, you do not lose.

Sir David Jason, OBE

Actor

'Look, learn, mark, inwardly digest.'

I found this little mantra particularly useful when I was a struggling, unknown actor. I was lucky enough to work with some fantastic characters who happened to be very talented people, such as Ron Moody, Bob Monkhouse, Ronnie Barker. I used to observe them avidly and analyse their particular style of delivery and acting in order to improve my own knowledge of timing and to find out what entertained an audience. By watching other performers, applying myself to my profession and being driven by my ambition, I found success in my own right. I am sure this is true of most professions and I've always found this quotation a neat little way of reminding myself to always strive for the highest standards in my work.

Digby, Lord Jones of Birmingham Kt

Director-General of the Confederation of British Industry 2000–2006;
UK Minister of State for Trade & Investment 2007–2008.

—— FORMULA FOR SUCCESS ——

Treat others as you would like to be treated. Life is far too important to be taken too seriously. It's very difficult to give a bollocking to a cheerful person! Don't do second.

—— INSIGHTS ——

If you fail because someone's better than you – lick your wounds, learn from the experience and move on. If you fail because you were complacent, you didn't prepare or you didn't work hard enough – never forgive yourself.

Give people time. Be sensitive to how they're thinking and feeling. Be tough but fair; there are always two sides to every issue. Never close your mind to either side.

Communicate, communicate, communicate; a little and often (even when you really don't feel like it) far outweighs none followed by 'initiatives'.

Be yourself, warts 'n all. People like being led by genuine people even if they are imperfect!

Never be frightened of asking why. No one expects you to know everything.

Surround yourself with clever people, support them, drive them on, give them public credit; work them hard but no harder than you work yourself and never ask them to do something they know you won't do yourself.

Be there to take the flak and protect the vulnerable, even if they are actually to blame – sort that out in private!

—— ANECDOTE ——

For God's sake – laugh! It's good for the team but also it's good for you. I served in the Royal Navy from 1974–1977. On one project, four of us had been training for it together. Three of us were getting on fine (even me!) but the fourth was a bit of a dud. All through the training we laughed at him (we were all 19 or 20 years old) as he constantly cocked things up. Come the day of delivery, the three of us sailed through but he failed. However we were being judged and marked as a team so we came last. Our Fleet Chief Petty Officer bollocked us sky high! It was a dressing-down I will never forget. It reduced me to tears. I feel ashamed even now 34 years on as I type this. 'Of course you're good,' he said (I use the word 'said' loosely!). 'You wouldn't be here if you weren't. We weren't judging how good you were at doing the stuff, we were looking for how you dealt with the guy who was not very good, how you brought him on, how you gave him confidence, how you made him feel good, got him to believe in himself; in short ... could you lead?! I never ever forgot that day. It changed me. People are kind enough to say I'm good with people; that day all those years ago is one of the reasons why.

—— INSPIRATIONAL QUOTATION ——

Taking a few lines of Rudyard Kipling out of order:

If you can meet with Triumph and Disaster,
And treat those two imposters just the same.
If you can talk with crowds nor lose your virtue,
Or walk with kings nor lose the common touch.
If neither foe nor loving friend can hurt you,
If all men count with you, but none too much.

—— FINAL THOUGHTS ——

As you look at successful people and wonder, question, perhaps admire, remember that in every case:

❖ There is a rock they somehow and somewhere depend on.

❖ There is a residual insecurity that constantly drives them on.

❖ They have the hardest taskmaster ever – themselves!

❖ They understand and live the fact that no matter how easy they make it look, life is not a breeze. The hard work, the hours and days of preparation, the constant nagging of the self-imposed quest for self-improvement – all go into the mix every day to deliver success.

Doreen Lawrence, OBE

Director, Stephen Lawrence Charitable Trust

My involvement with 'success' is an involuntary and tragic one. I have been unsuccessful in bringing, my son, Stephen's murderers to justice, after a 15-year campaign, although my quest continues. Some might argue that I have had some success in campaigning to change British justice and police procedures.

What is important to me now is that there is a legacy for Stephen and that his terrible murder should be a springboard to success for underprivileged young people so that they can achieve the dream he was denied. That is the aim of the Charitable Trust of which I am Director. I have tried to identify what personal characteristics might have helped me in my work.

My early years in the Caribbean have given me the grounding and self worth that has carried me through those dark days after the murder of my son. As a child I remember my grandmother who was like a tall Amazonian woman who walked proud. She was respected by all in the Clarendon district where she lived in Jamaica; she commanded respect without the need to be domineering. There was calmness about her and I felt safe as a child.

I believe that I have inherited my grandmother's calmness. Against the odds I challenged the justice system without fear. I am not fazed by those who hold power. Drawing on the strength from within and hearing my grandmother's voice whenever I doubt or question the obstacles that are placed before me.

I have the ability to engage in key areas of Government and I have contributed to change in the race relations law in the UK (Race Relation Amendment Act 2000). I have shown leadership within a diverse community. It has been necessary to have energy and resilience to champion and deliver goals and these traits balanced with the political influencing skills and sensitivity to promote change including winning hearts and minds. I like to think that I am an effective networker and ambassador. Others tell me that I have the ability to command confidence and credibility both internally and externally.

Over the years I have proven that strength of character and determination actually come from within and are not things that can be taught. I truly believe that we all have this strength and we just need to believe in ourselves and stay focussed.

I admire Maya Angleou and her poem, *Still I Rise*:

'You may write me down in history
With your bitter, twisted lies,
You may trod me in the very dirt
But still, like dust, I'll rise.'

With all the struggle over the years I think this poem reflects what it was like for me at the time of Stephen's death (and in some ways still is).

Maureen Lipman,
CBE, Hon DLitt (Hull), Hon MA (Salford), Hon DLitt (Sheffield)

Actress, writer, Professor of Drama (Sheffield University)

In my overcrowded business, it's not enough to have talent. You also have to get the job.

Kenneth Tynan famously said of Laurence Olivier:

> 'He spent thirty seconds working out what you wanted him to be, and ten seconds becoming it.'

This approach will get you the job, but it doesn't tie in with my other maxim which is 'Become what you are.' I think this is probably the saying of a Buddhist leader. Two contradictory statements but both of them are separately aspirational and perhaps what they say together is that we all have many aspects to our personalities and life is a journey towards using the right qualities for the right ends.

I have been inspired by my high school teacher Joan Nicholson, who gave me the part of Dr. Faustus, at the age of thirteen, at an all girls school in Hull. Also, because the following year she cast me as Margaret, the serving woman in *Much Ado About Nothing*, when I would have been a cracking Beatrice, because the success of my Dr. Faustus had gone to my head. A good lesson for the future.

Hilaire Belloc said: 'Hate is a coward's revenge for being intimidated.' I think of that every time I read a first night review. I also believe in the power of love and particularly of friendship and that both have to be constantly worked on and revitalised.

I believe that music is sublime and can cut through reason to a place we often have no time to acknowledge. 'I am not interested in the pursuit of happiness,' wrote Joyce Grenfell, 'but only in the discovery of joy.'

I also love the dark lyrics of Lorenz Hart. Here's one from 'It never entered my mind':

> 'You have what I lack myself, Now I even have to scratch my back myself.'

Bereavement has taught me that there is only one way to handle loss and that is your own way. For me it was work, my kids and poetry. Writing my grief into wryness always helps and of course that is strongly the Jewish experience. I am intensely proud of my northern roots and my Jewish ones and the tribe of artists amongst whom I live and work. And I'm so lucky to be in a profession with no time limit on my usefulness.

Air Chief Marshal Sir Clive Loader, KCB, OBE, ADC, FRAeS, RAF

Commander-in-Chief, Royal Air Force

—— FORMULA FOR SUCCESS ——

Professionalism must underpin all. Using that skill, plan ahead but be prepared to change the plan when Question 4 ('Has Something Changed?') applies.

—— INSIGHTS ——

There is only one thing worse than making a mistake, and that is continuing with the original course once you have realised the error; have both the humility and the courage to admit the error and then (realigned) move on (hopefully, still with your people…).

You are not as great as you think you are and others are generally better than you credit them as being. Indeed, in a quiet moment, you might even be prepared to admit that you are yourself lucky to be where you are. So, given that you have two ears and one mouth, make sure you use them in that ratio. Have fun and be ruthlessly honest – the first will rub off on those around you, and failure with the second will bring your downfall quicker than you could possibly imagine.

—— INSPIRATIONAL QUOTATION ——

'The great thing about not planning ahead is that failure comes as a complete surprise rather than being preceded by a period of worry and depression.' (Sir John Harvey-Jones)

Allan Middleton, FRSA, MIFL, DIPPC, DMS, Cert ED, PCEP

Multiple award winner: The Butler Trust Development Award; The Fleur Lombard Award; The Youth Justice Board Communication and Media Award; The Fire Service Partnership of the year Award; The Merrill Lynch Raising Achievement in young people award; Public Servant of the year award 2006

—— CAREER/POSITION ——

Crew Manager, Avon Fire & Rescue Service, February 1979 to date.

—— INSIGHT ——

Ever despondent at the amount of anti-social behaviour displayed by young people, I developed a Youth Engagement Programme that operates inside a young offenders prison. In order to further develop the scheme, I have been seconded to HMP and YOI Ashfield. There has been massive interest in my scheme nationwide.

It is apparent that young people today are growing up without boundaries, or without realising and accepting that there are consequences for their actions and behaviour.

Using my 29 years experience as a fire fighter, I engage with young people to deliver workshops and courses.

I ensure there is a behavioural contract from the outset. The contract is made by all involved and applies to both the young people and myself. They are informed that if the contract is broken there will always be an immediate sanction.

I never shy from challenging unacceptable or confrontational behaviour.

As a positive role model for these impressionable and often vulnerable young people, I always ensure that I am consistent. I will be the same today as I was yesterday and will be tomorrow. The same rules apply today, yesterday and tomorrow. The aim is to help young people discover their own potential and turn their backs on anti-social behaviour and crime.

'With the correct help and support young people can turn their lives around. After all it is they who will shape all our futures one way or another.'

My courses and workshops give young people a constructive insight into the real world where I make use of pictures and video footage taken at incidents. These give the young people the opportunity to witness first hand the devastation and consequences of other people's actions.

The courses also provide young people with lots of skills and discipline, and encourage much needed self-esteem. Discipline without bullying equals respect. Some of the young people become assistants and help me to run the courses.

When they are confident I take them to schools to talk to other disaffected young people who are on the edge of exclusion.

I firmly believe that mentoring is a powerful tool for rehabilitation. I have developed a nationwide mentoring scheme to ensure that young people receive mentoring whilst held within a secure estate. This can continue upon their release; because the young people know and like the Fire Service, they trust and respect these mentors.

Success is something that needs to be worked at despite the obstacles and jealousy put in your way. What inspires me is the end result of changing mindsets and attitudes of these young people. One former Ashfield inmate is now employed by Avon Fire & Rescue Service as a Youth Advocate.

—— INSPIRATION ——

My biggest inspiration to do this work was due to having attended numerous road traffic collisions, arson attacks and witnessing personal tragedies evolving before my eyes. Giving talks in schools to young people inspired me and made me want to take this further and make it work.

I really feel for the victims of crime; if we can stop these young people committing further crimes when they are released from prison that will mean fewer victims. My courses have been designed to include victims and I ensure that the young people hear first-hand accounts directly from victims.

—— INSPIRATIONAL QUOTATION ——

'Give me the boy and I will show you the man.' (St Ignatius of Loyola)

Sir Patrick Moore, CBE, FRS

Writer, astronomer and broadcaster [and self-taught composer]

Dogged determination and decisiveness.

Success? Well as a writer and astronomer and broadcaster I suppose I claim to be mildly successful – at any rate. I have produced over a hundred books – and in the words of the old song, I did it 'my way'. But I was in an unusual situation, because I was on my own, so that if everything went wrong it wouldn't affect anyone but me. (I hate to bother readers with personal details, but I must give one note, because if I don't what follows would make no sense at all. In 1943 my fiancée was killed by a German bomb, so marriage was 'out'.)

My recipe: Decide what you want to do; go for it 100%, and – this is vital – do not change course if things do not pan out straight away. Well-meaning people may try to divert you, but if, deep down, you know the career you would really enjoy, keep pegging away; it will work in the end. I took a gamble. I well remember my first 'Sky at Night' TV broadcast, in April 1957. All television was live in those days. The announcement flashed up on the screen in front of me, and I thought: 'My real career depends on what I do in the next twenty minutes.' I suppose it did. [His appearances on this programme led to Moore becoming the world's longest serving television presenter (*Guinness Book of Records*).]

So may I give two recommendations: First; follow the career you want and enjoy and ignore all attempts at diversion. Secondly; when you want to take action, ask yourself two questions: (a) Is it sensible? (b) Will it cause hurt or distress to anyone? If the answers are (a) Yes and (b) No, do it. If not – don't.

—— INSPIRATIONAL QUOTATION ——

'We will never surrender.' (WINSTON CHURCHILL)

(Tell that to Mr. Brown.)

Quote by Sir Patrick Moore (on the Monster Raving Loony Party):

> 'They had one advantage over all the other parties. They knew they were loonies.' (OBSERVER 1999)

Sir Stirling Moss, OBE, FIE

*Ex-racing driver, now company director, landlord
and in PR, flogging a fading image!*

—— PERSONAL FORMULA FOR SUCCESS ——

Concentration, feeling of balance, efficiency and honesty.

—— INSIGHT ——

Who inspired me? My father had a great influence on my life and outlook
on same. He was both my friend and mentor. He was with me every step
of the way and the standards and determination that I learnt from him all
those years ago, I continue to live by today.

—— MY FAVOURITE SAYING? ——

Actually, there are two of them by which I live and raced:

'Movement is tranquillity.'

'I would rather lose a race driving fast enough to win it, than win a
race driving slowly enough to lose it!'

Sir Paul Nurse, FRS, PHD

Biochemist, President of Rockefeller University, Awarded the Nobel Prize for Medicine (2001), the French Legion d'Honneur (2002), the Copley Medal (2005, Former Director General Cancer Research UK)

—— FORMULA FOR SUCCESS ——

Success = Curiosity + pursuit of knowledge + intellectual endeavour + valuing the alternative + good fortune.

Of these success elements I would highlight the last one. Let me explain by giving a few examples of how good fortune came into my early life.

I was very lucky to be brought up in a loving, happy working class family by, as it turned out, my grandparents (I only found out at age 57 that my 'parents' were actually my grandparents – how ironic that even though I am a geneticist, my family managed to keep my genetic origins secret from me for over half a century.)

Before me nobody from the family had ever been to university and therefore they adopted an alternative view in supporting my academic efforts and aspirations both at school and university. We lived first in Norfolk before moving to Wembley where, I remember, the long walks I had to make, often alone, to get to and from my primary school. This walk took me through a park and some rough land where I could not fail to notice the animals, insects and plants there and how they changed during the seasons. During the winter my attention was attracted to the changes in the stars and planets in the sky. Two incidents from this time that I remember were, wondering why leaves were larger on plants growing in the shade compared with the same plants growing in sunlight, and watching Sputnik 2, the second ever artificial satellite and the first with a living cargo (a dog called Laika), as it sped across the skies of London. My life-long interest in astronomy started then.

My primary school teachers made the world seem such an interesting place and encouraged my innate curiosity but I also see this walk as being a catalyst in awakening my early interest in science. I sometimes wonder what would have happened in my life if I had been bussed to school.

My second bit of luck was in being taught by an excellent Biology teacher at my secondary school, Harrow County Grammar School for Boys. Moving to this academic state school was a mixed experience for me. It was a good, well-resourced school, but was very exam-oriented and most of the other boys came from wealthier and more academic families which sometimes made me feel like a fish out of water. I was never very good at exams, having a poor memory and finding the examination process rather artificial, and there never seemed to be enough time to follow up things that really interested me. But I was fortunate to have Keith Neal as biology teacher – he encouraged his pupils to study natural history and do real experiments. I was also lucky to meet some good friends and be introduced to extra-curricular activities which I have followed through my life.

Providence struck a third time after I left school. At first I was not able to attend university because, although I had achieved examination grades which allowed me to get into university, I did not have the basic language qualification which at the time was compulsory for all university entrants. Unfortunately, I continued to fail my French exam and it was only the intervention of Professor Jinks at Birmingham University that got me into university. Fortuitively he had noticed my application for entry and asked me to visit his Genetics Department. After an extensive interview he arranged for my weaknesses in foreign languages to be overlooked and so I started a Biology degree at Birmingham in 1967.

My time as an undergraduate at Birmingham was extremely stimulating both as a biologist and also for my more general intellectual development. It was the heady times of the 60s when everything could be challenged and everything seemed possible. I had an eccentric zoology tutor, Jack Cohen, who was hugely stimulating and entertaining, and although frequently wrong was always wrong in an interesting way. He taught me the value of the alternative view. For the first time I fully recognised the excitement of intellectual endeavour and realised that this was what I wanted to do with my life.

A most important example of my luck is that it was at Birmingham that I met my wife Anne who was a sociology student, and her influence together with activities associated with the student movement of the time opened up my interests amongst other things into the theatre, art, music, politics and philosophy. Again luckily she shared my desire to be at the cutting edge of research, helping to save lives without the constraint of the market – rather than going into industry and becoming a multimillionaire. Anne and I created our two beautiful daughters, Sarah and Emily, my final example of pure good fortune.

Bruce Oldfield, OBE

British Couture Dress Designer of 35 years standing
and Vice President, Barnado's

—— FORMULA FOR SUCCESS ——

Success requires a certain detachment from people, an instinct for survival, an unswerving yet well-evaluated belief in your personal abilities and the necessary flexibility to respond positively and speedily to obstacles.

—— INSIGHT ——

I am always surprised when people remark on how successful I have been. I find it hard to quantify. I'm not extremely rich; certainly couldn't fund a jet-set lifestyle (not something that I've ever aspired to). My achievement might be that I've reached almost 60 and still feel that I have lots that I want to do with my career and, importantly, that I have the energy to still pursue it and an audience that continues to want it.

I suppose that the single most important factor contributing to my success has been my unwillingness to accept the pretty uninspiring pattern that was laid out for me at a fairly young age due to my background in care. What others labelled as cockiness and arrogance I shrugged off as self-belief. To this day (although my goals and aspirations have been tempered with time), I remain convinced that I still have what it takes to go further. That's why I still enjoy what I do.

—— INSPIRATIONAL POEM ——

'The Road Not Taken' (ROBERT FROST)

TWO roads diverged in a yellow wood,
And sorry I could not travel both
And be one traveler, long I stood
And looked down one as far as I could
To where it bent in the undergrowth;

Then took the other, as just as fair,
And having perhaps the better claim,
Because it was grassy and wanted wear;
Though as for that the passing there
Had worn them really about the same,

And both that morning equally lay
In leaves no step had trodden black.
Oh, I kept the first for another day!
Yet knowing how way leads on to way,
I doubted if I should ever come back.

I shall be telling this with a sigh
Somewhere ages and ages hence:
Two roads diverged in a wood, and I—
I took the one less travelled by,
And that has made all the difference.

Jeremy Paxman

Broadcaster, journalist, author.

I have no 'formula': I just – as Churchill said – 'keep buggering on.'

Jonathon Porritt, CBE

Founder Director of Forum for the Future, Chairman of the UK Sustainable Development Commission and author of 'Capitalism as if the World Matters' (Earthscan Publications Ltd)

—— CAREER INSIGHT ——

My professional career started out 35 years ago when I took up a post as teacher of English and Drama in a West London Comprehensive School – and simultaneously found myself getting involved in The Green Party (or The Ecology Party as it was then). Ten years later, in 1984, I left teaching to become Director of Friends of the Earth. I thought at the time that I would probably go back into teaching after a few years!

As it happens, I'm still in teaching – just in a rather different way. As far as today's sustainable development agenda is concerned, there is still a lot of explaining and persuading to be done, of advocating and navigating, of inspiring and catalysing, of empowering and exhorting – all good teaching skills! Just because more and more things now fit directly under the 'blindingly obvious' category of what should or shouldn't happen, that doesn't mean to say that they will happen.

And that's really what I end up doing, day in day out, under the aegis of Forum for the Future (an educational charity I set up back in 1994), The Sustainable Development Commission (where I have been Chairman for 8 years), The Prince of Wales's Business and Environment Programme (which I helped set up 12 years ago, and of which I remain co-Director), and as a Board Member of the South West Regional Development Agency and at the water company, Wessex Water.

—— FORMULA FOR SUCCESS ——

Stay angry, keep smiling, celebrate life – every day – and never give up.

—— INSIGHT INTO FORMULA ——

Not everybody would go with the 'angry' bit. But if you are not angry at the devastation that we are inflicting on the earth, at the harm we do each other, at the soul-less banality and cruelty that shapes so many people's lives, and at the way in which we are crushing the future life chances of our children, then you're just not living on the same planet as I am. And it is going to get a lot worse fast if we don't start turning things around very soon. So that's where the anger comes in!

—— TIP FOR SUCCESS ——

At the risk of sounding pretentious (simply because I don't really have a simple 'tip for success!'), I first got stuck in on sustainability issues all those years ago when I realised that what mattered most in life wasn't me stumbling through it, with all the usual ups and downs, pluses and minuses, but the way life was surging through me. From then on, I have just had a very simple, practical sense of what 'interdependence' really means – as in what is perhaps the most eloquent of the 27 Principles embodied in the 1992 Rio Declaration: 'Peace, Development and Environmental Protection are interdependent and indivisible.' Somehow, though, I really don't quite know how, it just *does* all connect as far as I'm concerned: causes, people, the rest of life on Earth, the big cosmological stuff and the tiny little details.

—— INSPIRATIONAL QUOTATION ——

'We must do what we conceive to be the right thing, and not bother our heads or burden our souls with whether we are going to be successful. Because if we don't do the right thing, we will be doing the wrong thing, and we'll just be part of the disease and not part of the cure.' (FRITZ SCHUMAKER, *Small is Beautiful*)

—— FINAL THOUGHT ——

I actually hate having to talk about 'success' as some off-the-shelf product that can be delivered into any old organisation, or a set of attributes and behaviours that can be taught to people. Hence my nervousness about 'leadership courses' and my contempt for DIY leadership books! At its simplest, if you can be fully yourself, and help make it possible for other people to be fully themselves, then that is probably close to practical leadership as we are ever likely to get.

Baroness Prashar of Runneymede, CBE

Chairman of the Judicial Appointments Commission, Chairman of the Royal Commonwealth Society, Non-Executive Director of the ITV Board, Non-Executive Director of the Cabinet Office, Governor The Ditchley Foundation, Governor of Ashridge College, Trustee of Miriam Rothschild and John Foster Trust, Member The Advisory Board, Youth at Risk, Chair The Advisory Board, Centre for Parliamentary Studies, Patron of the Runnymede Trust, Patron of Opportunity and Grace Foundation.

Former roles include; First Civil Service Commission, Executive Chairman of the Parole Board of England and Wales, Director of the National Council for Voluntary Organisation and Director of the Runnymede Trust, Chancellor De Montfort University, Chairman of the National Literacy Trust, Non-Executive Director at UNITE plc, Trustee of the BBC World Service Trust, member of the Commission on Women and the Criminal Justice System

—— FORMULA FOR SUCCESS ——

Do the right thing for the right reasons. This brings focus, clarity and ensures an ethical approach.

—— INSIGHT ——

There is only one success – to be able to spend your life in your own way. I have always remained focussed and true to my beliefs and standards but open to learning and constantly improving myself. Humility and perseverance are important as is the ability to have fun. Those who have given their services to others, particularly the disadvantaged, inspire me.

—— INSPIRATIONAL QUOTATION ——

'It has always been a mystery to me how men can feel themselves honoured by the humiliation of their fellow beings.' (MAHATMA GANDHI)

Libby Purves, OBE

Novelist, journalist and broadcaster

—— FORMULA FOR SUCCESS ——

I think it was George Orwell who said 'Every life, seen from within, is a succession of small defeats.' He was right. The knack of reaching comparative success is to try not to be cast down by this feeling. Enjoy the good bits and forget the bad ones.

Sir Steve Redgrave, CBE, DL

Rower and winner of five Olympic gold medals

—— FORMULA FOR SUCCESS ——

Some people train to win; I train to eliminate the possibility of defeat.

I have always tried to put my previous success out of my mind. As I advise business and sports people when giving motivational talks, 'You never win with last year's performance.'

Sir Stuart Rose

Executive Chairman, Marks and Spencer plc,
Chairman Business in the Community

—— CAREER ——

I began my career in retail at Marks & Spencer in 1972 before going on to the Burton Group in 1989, becoming Chief Executive of the Multiples Division in 1994. I was Chief Executive of Argos plc in 1998 and later became Chief Executive of Booker plc. Before re-joining Marks & Spencer as Chief Executive in 2004 (and then becoming Executive Chairman in June 2008), I was Chief Executive of Arcadia Group plc from 2000 until 2002. I am a non-executive director of Land Securities plc.

I am also Appeal Chairman of The Healing Foundation. The Healing Foundation is a national fundraising charity established to champion the cause of people living with disfigurement and visible loss of function.

—— FORMULA FOR SUCCESS ——

A personal favourite of mine is: 'If you do not look out of the window every day, when you finally do the world has passed you by.'

—— INSIGHTS ——

From a retail perspective, I've always tried to stick to the principles outlined by a former Chairman, Lord Marcus Sieff. He summarised these principles as:

❖ Offer customers a selected range of high quality, well designed and attractive merchandise at reasonable prices which represent good value

❖ Simplify operational procedures so the business runs effectively

❖ Foster good human relations with staff, customers and suppliers.

Lord Sieff learnt these principles in the early 50s. They are as relevant today as they were then.

I've always had a soft spot for 'You'll Never Walk Alone', not that I'm a fan of Liverpool FC.

> When you walk through a storm
> Hold your head up high
> And don't be afraid of the dark
> At the end of the storm
> Is a golden sky
> And the sweet silver song of the lark

These lyrics were especially relevant when I returned to the business in 2004. We had a lot to do to turn things round but we always felt there was light at the end of the tunnel.

—— OTHER TIPS ——

There are a couple of additional tips that have always served me well.

Firstly, I find a lot of business is about getting people working together as a team and all pointing in the same direction. And then articulating in one, two, three simple sentences what the business is about.

Secondly, I use the phrase 'restless dissatisfaction' with my teams. If they come in with a sense of restless dissatisfaction then it gives them an extra impetus to push on. I imagine athletes to be similar. A sprinter might run the 100m in 10 seconds but you can bet he wouldn't be satisfied. He'd be determined to get to 9.99 seconds next time out.

Rt Hon Alex Salmond, MSP MP

First Minister of Scotland

—— FORMULA FOR SUCCESS ——

90% perspiration; 10% inspiration.

—— INSPIRATION ——

A source of inspiration can be found in setting goals and achieving them. I believe that Scotland is ready for change and for reform. This is a small nation with a big future. But it is also a small nation with big challenges. I look forward to meeting those challenges as First Minister of the Scottish Government and continuing to articulate the case for an Independent Scotland.

—— QUOTATION ——

'Work as if you live in the early days of a better nation.'

A quote by the Scottish writer, Alasdair Gray, used in various pieces of his work. I used this in my address at Prestonfield House Hotel on 4 May 2007 when it became apparent that the Scottish National Party had won their first ever election.

Dame Marjorie Scardino

Chief Executive, Pearson plc

There is no one formula for success; in fact, there is no one way even to measure success. In business, there are a bundle of familiar measures.

—— INSIGHTS ——

As the chief executive of a public company, I recite just a few of them when we announce our financial results each year: revenues, operating profit, return on invested capital, earnings per share.

But in a company whose work is centred on education, journalism and books, we're lucky enough to be working for something larger than ourselves. And our success can finally be measured only by the reaction of the people who use our products to help make progress in their lives intellectually and practically. Success on the financial measures for our company is a by-product of our customers' personal success.

The same goes for an individual. Working for something larger than yourself tends to be more satisfying, and it has important by-products. But because it requires you to balance the financial rewards, which sustain an enterprise or a family, and the subjective rewards of that larger purpose, which defines a human being, it's hard to be precise about the rules for achieving it.

Luck – or fortuity –often plays a part, or seems to. Of course you can create conditions that make you attractive to luck. I attribute any success I've enjoyed to a good education and a passion for reading, and then to generous people who took a chance on me. From those chances, I learned other lessons that are generally so homespun they are familiar to every school boy and girl. But they've been important to me. Here's one of them:

Back in the 1980s, my husband and I started a small local newspaper in the US – in Savannah, Georgia. It was called *The Georgia Gazette*. And while we didn't have many reporters, or much money, what we did have was a determination to help move our community along. So we scoured public records, and chased interviews, and developed a few stories that helped reveal how city and state governments conducted their business in ways that were bad for citizens. That to me was real success – the satisfaction that what the newspaper wrote really mattered to its readers.

We didn't have economic success, though. After eight years we had to close the newspaper, as the economics of competing (and our lack of deep knowledge about how to run a business) left an imbalance between our sales and our costs. You might say we failed; and we did fail commercially. But our editorial contribution to the community helped make it better; and what we learned about business was more valuable than any MBA. But the most important result of our experience was that we lost our fear of failure. We failed, and we didn't die. That has been an asset to me throughout my business life.

One person who has inspired me over the years is Walter Bagehot, who was editor in the mid-19th century of *The Economist*, the weekly publication half-owned by Pearson. Fourteen volumes of Bagehot's writings stay on the bookshelf in my office, and *The Economist*'s weekly column on British politics is to this day called 'Bagehot', because his unique take on that subject still informs us.

Walter Bagehot had his bit of luck: it didn't hurt that he married the daughter of the newspaper's founder. But it was talent, wisdom and perseverance – not luck – that produced the classic books for which he's best known and that moved *his* community along: *The English Constitution* and *Lombard Street*. And it was those personal characteristics that have inspired me, not least his ability to state household truths in a memorable way.

It was Walter Bagehot who said: 'The greatest pleasure in life is doing what other people say you cannot do.' Having the courage to try it, and to learn from the setbacks, is a success in itself.

Sir Martin Sorrell

Businessman, CEO WPP. Member of Council for Excellence in Management and Leadership and Member of the Committee for the Special Olympics. Deputy Chairman and Governor, London Business School, a member of the Advisory Boards of the Judge Business School and IESE and member of the Dean's Council for Boston University. Chairman of the Global Advisory Board of the Centre for International Business and Management (Cambridge University). Member of the Board of Directors of Harvard Business School and of the Board of the Indian School of Business.

—— FORMULA FOR SUCCESS ——

Think; make work your life; be precise; pay attention to detail and embrace change.

—— INSIGHT 1 ——

I like to think about things. In my work I profited from taking this approach and from the focus, intensity and determination that I'd gained from my time at Harvard. Harvard's hothouse atmosphere stayed with me. Fear of failure drove me. But the trouble was we were made to feel that we could run the world.

—— INSIGHT 2 ——

I don't regard what I do as being work. That's the difference between somebody who founds a business and somebody that manages it or is a hired hand. I don't regard myself as a manager. The attachment I have with WPP is more emotional than that, more akin to physically giving birth. I always think of the Bill Shankly quote about football not being a matter of life and death but more important than that. It's the same for me with WPP.

—— INSIGHT 3 ——

Being precise and knowing your business in some detail are important success traits. When asked what their revenues, costs, profits and cashflow are, few respond coherently. The odds of success are still 1 in 100, as General Doriot [founder of the American Research and Development Corporation, the first publicly owned venture capital firm] used to say: 'Sometimes it seems that sardines are for buying and selling, not for eating.'

As long as the old farts (like me) at the top of the company do not prevent change, it's fine. If they do you're in trouble. Shortage of human capital will be one of the main challenges facing companies in the future and corporate success will depend on finding, retaining and incentivising good people. There are significant changes in the attitudes of young people. They understand the need for change and they would rather work in smaller less bureaucratic companies. In order to accommodate these sentiments, the way we organise our companies is on a tribal basis, so WPP is not one homogenous, elephantine company. It's a group of a hundred or so tribes. What we're seeking to do is to capitalise on the benefits of scale, with the heart, mind, soul and energy of a small company.

—— MY PERSONAL CREDO ——

'Persistence and speed.'

—— MY PREFERRED EPITAPH ——

'The person who initiated the growth of the best advertising and marketing services company in the world.'

Dame Barbara Stocking, CBE

Chief Executive, Oxfam GB

My career is about leading organisations of purpose and passion. Oxfam is a major humanitarian, development and campaigning agency that believes we can end poverty in the world.

—— FORMULA FOR SUCCESS ——

Do what you said you will do – as much in small things as in large.

—— FORMULA EXPLAINED ——

People often say I am a good networker. I do enjoy people, but I think it is also about being helpful and delivering what you have said.

—— INSPIRATIONAL LEADER ——

One person who continues to inspire me is Kofi Annan, previously UN Secretary General. It is partly because of his commitment to ending poverty and to reducing conflict in the world. As important is his ability to have 'grace under pressure'. He was severely attacked by the US in his last period at the UN, but he withstood that pressure with great dignity. It's a lesson about not letting things get to you, but going ahead committed to your cause.

—— QUOTATION ——

'Be the change you want to see in the world.' (MAHATMA GHANDI)

—— ONE LAST THOUGHT ——

I think one important thing in [successful] leadership is to respect people . and I don't just mean staff, but also in our case the people who live in poverty, and the public. The latter have more sense than they are credited for.

Sir Arnold Wesker, FRSL

Playwright

I think a distinction must be made between 'success' and 'achievement'. Successful I am not, but in terms of output as a writer it has to be acknowledged that I have achieved a substantial body of work behind me. What I'm saying is that I'm famous but broke, and have always lived on an overdraft!

How, therefore, can I put forward a 'personal formula for success'? My problem is that I left out the 'z' in Einstein's equation ($A=x+y+z$), where A is success, x is work, y is play and z is knowing when to keep your mouth shut – I didn't know when to keep my mouth shut!

But when students or aspiring playwrights ask for advice I offer them two pieces: one is cynical: go into business first and build yourself a 'f***-you fund'; the other is serious and rooted in experience: be persistent.

The generally accepted wisdom is 'be true to yourself' but I would not categorically put that forward as a virtue since being true to one's self might involve conflict with the powers that be who don't share your truths.

Einstein's advice is more practical if damaging to self-esteem: keep your mouth shut!

But again one must make distinctions. True to yourself in behaviour or in your writing? Being true to yourself in behaviour – not advisable. Being true to yourself in the way you write and about what you write – essential.

It's also difficult to be specific about 'success' when so much depends upon luck – being the right person at the right time in the right place. Perhaps it's useful to suggest to young writers that they be alert to what could be the right time and the right place; the ability to recognise the right time and the right place might be what makes them the right person!

And then there's 'the helping hand'. I was lucky to meet a young film/ stage director attached to the Royal Court Theatre, Lindsay Anderson, who agreed to read my first play which he admired and promoted to the Court. I don't know how you can guide a young person to find such a helping hand.

Is there enough there to constitute 'a formula for success? Perhaps the hard truth is that there exists no one formula for success, perhaps no formula at all. Perhaps the truth about 'success' resides in the person him/her self. Some have got it, some haven't.

And who's to say 'success' is so desirable, anyway? The ability to earn a living might be gratifying but the need to be successful might lead to ugliness. Ugliness of spirit and personality I mean. I'm not suggesting people should be satisfied with their lot; human drive, imagination and innovation is needed to turn the world but so is the selflessness of humanitarian aid workers. I've always been wary of the idea of 'The Top Ten'. It is true that there exist major writers and minor ones, but some of the so called 'minor' ones have provided such great pleasure and illumination that I feel the concept of 'The Top Ten' or 'The 90 greats' is retrogressive.

Finally, I like the story of the young couple in New York late for a concert who stop an old lady asking: 'Excuse us, but how do we get to Carnegie Hall, please?' Replied the old lady: 'Practise, practise, practise.'

Jonny Wilkinson, OBE

Rugby union player and in England's 2003 Rugby World Cup winning team

'Be the change you want to see.'

'Failing at something is one thing, but Buddhism tells us that it is up to us how we interpret that failure. The so-called Middle Way is about seeing everything as interconnected success and failure, victory and defeat. Who is to say that the foundations of success in the 2003 World Cup were not built on the failures that went before? The Middle Way is also about having the right intentions. Are they decent and honest and are you giving consideration to other people? Selfishness can never be the route to happiness or success.' (*Times*, 19 September 2008)

Michael Winner, MA (Cantab), OBE (offered, but rejected)

Film Producer, Director, Writer, Journalist, Author, TV Appearer
and General Nuisance

—— FORMULA FOR SUCCESS ——

Never give up.

—— CAREER INSIGHT ——

I believe that success is not necessarily to the fleet of foot but to those who persevere, accept and stand firm when rejected, but continue undaunted. When I came down from Cambridge aged 20 with an Honours Degree in Law and Economics, I thought the film world would be waiting for me eagerly. Not surprisingly, this did not turn out to be true. I wrote endless letters seeking employment at the lowest level. Very few of these letters were answered. When they were answered at least I could look at the notepaper even if they said, 'We don't have anything, go away.'

I can trace my entire career back to an evening when I went to see a film called *The Enemy Below* starring Robert Mitchum and Kurt Jurgens at the Carlton Cinema in Lower Regent Street.

In those days they ran short films before the main film. A documentary about Ireland was already on the screen when I got into my seat. When it finished it said, 'The End – a Harold Baim Production'. I thought, 'That's someone I have not written to.' So I wrote to Mr Baim seeking employment. Four weeks later I was sitting at home and Harold Baim telephoned me and said, 'Are you busy?' At the time I was looking out of the window watching buses go by. To say I was not busy was a gross understatement.

Mr Baim offered me a job as an Associate Producer on a documentary to be made about the Air Force and Navy on an aircraft carrier called HMS Victorious. My job was to generally carry bits of camera around and occasionally assist in whatever manner I could. The unit consisted of three people: Harold Baim, who produced and directed, me; a general dogsbody; and a camera man who carried a bottle of scotch in his pocket and was permanently somewhat pissed.

From these humble beginnings I met other people. The camera man introduced me to another company making films and thus I got into feature films. But I can trace it all back to Harold Baim who was an extremely nice man for whom I made many short films before going on to making feature films on Hollywood and all over the world.

'No good turn goes unpunished.'

Sir Clive Woodward, OBE

Director of Elite Performance British Olympic Association, former Coach of England World Cup winning rugby team, former international rugby player

100 things 1% better.

I am often asked for the 'magic formulae' or 'secret ingredient' that goes into creating a winning team or champion individual. It is difficult to sum up the elements that go into a winning organisation in a few words; it is simplest to say that there is no ONE great thing but very many that, when altogether, add up to making the difference between success or failure.

So 100 things 1% better becomes a mantra for the leader and the team. Everything comes under scrutiny. Imagine if you will an empty room – a clean, white space – then bring into the 'room' the things that you deem necessary for you to complete the core function of your business or sport. Only bring into the room the things that you need. Now look at them closer; could they be bettered?; could you do them another, more successful way?

For example, a rugby player needs kit, so bring back kit into the 'room'. But what is the kit like? Is it doing the right job for you? Can it be improved? Nike, the suppliers to the England kit in 2003, redesigned the playing strip for the England team – we wanted something tighter, more difficult to get hold of and a better fabric than an old style thick shirt. The new style strip was a huge success and has been copied around the world by other teams. Did England win a World Cup just because of their shirts? Of course not, but if you add up all of the '1%ers', as I call them, you have a team that is operating on a different level.

Once you adopt this for your team it becomes part of the team culture and everyone positively questions how we can do this better. It is all about hard work, but fundamental to understanding how to change organisational thinking and drives standards up. In a sporting context it applies to the coaching and playing of the sport just as much, if not more, than the off-pitch organisation; it underpins everything that you do.

3
Insights Provided by Contemporary Britons

The following inspirational quotes, poems and insights were provided specifically for this anthology by people who wanted to support the book and its charitable aim but felt uncomfortable about the personal association with 'success' – from my experience in editing this book, a not uncommon British trait.

Lord Melvyn Bragg

Writer and broadcaster

I am particularly fond of this poem about a pilot in WWI:

An Irish Airman Foresees his Death (**W.B. YEATS**)

I KNOW that I shall meet my fate
Somewhere among the clouds above;
Those that I fight I do not hate
Those that I guard I do not love;
My country is Kiltartan Cross,
My countrymen Kiltartan's poor,
No likely end could bring them loss
Or leave them happier than before.
Nor law, nor duty bade me fight,
Nor public man, nor cheering crowds,
A lonely impulse of delight
Drove to this tumult in the clouds;
I balanced all, brought all to mind,
The years to come seemed waste of breath,
A waste of breath the years behind
In balance with this life, this death.

Rt Hon David Cameron MP

Leader of the Conservative Party and Leader of the Opposition

—— INSPIRATIONAL TEXT ——

'Ask not what your country can do for you – ask what you can do for your country.' (JOHN F. KENNEDY, inaugural address, 20 January 1961)

Lord Sebastian Coe, KBE

Chairman, the London Organising Committee of the Olympic Games and Paralympic Games; former athlete; Olympic Gold Medal winner

—— INSPIRATIONAL QUOTATION ——

'To adhere to standards, to idealism, to vision in the face of immediate dangers takes self-confidence. But we also know that only those who dare to fail greatly can ever achieve greatly.' (ROBERT F KENNEDY, 1966)

Charles Handy, CBE

Author, social philosopher and management educator

My very personal view of success can be summed up as follows: Uniqueness is all. We are, each of us, uniquely gifted in some way. To be all that you could be, and to use that for the good of others, is to be successful.

Dame Kelly Holmes

Dame Commander of the British Empire, BBC Sports Personality of the Year and Laureus World Sportswoman of the Year.

—— CAREER ——

In 2004, set a new UK record for the 1500m, but also won 'double gold' for both the 800m and the 1500m in the Olympics.

—— INSPIRATIONAL SONG ——

If I Ain't Got You (Alicia Keys).

—— INSIGHT ——

In the 2004 Olympics, this song meant everything to me. In my mind, the 'You' in the title and the words of the song were the medals that I was so determined to win.

At the Olympics, I used the song on every warm-up, and found myself humming it before every event. For me it is the ultimate piece of inspirational music.

Sir Tom Hunter

Philanthropist and businessman

'Making mistakes is all part of the framework. If people are too scared to make mistakes there will be no successes.' (Sir Tom Hunter)

'He who dies thus rich, dies disgraced.' (Andrew Carnegie)

Boris Johnson

Mayor of London. Journalist, author.
Former editor of the Spectator magazine and former MP.

'Always remember darling, it's not how you're doing, it's what you're doing.' (My grandmother)

Joanna Lumley

Actress

Sunset and evening star,
And one clear call for me!
And may there be no moaning of the bar,
When I put out to sea,
But such a tide as moving seems asleep,
Too full for sound and foam,
When that which drew from out the boundless deep
Turns again home.
Twilight and evening bell,
And after that the dark!
And may there be no sadness of farewell,
When I embark;
For tho' from out our bourne of Time and Place
The flood may bear me far,
I hope to see my Pilot face to face
When I have crossed the bar.

ALFRED LORD TENNYSON

John Ord

Poet

The Secret of Success (JOHN ORD)
'When young I often thought success,
Meant wealth and power I must stress,
An easy life, with all life's pleasures,
A mansion high, with worldly treasures,
Tours abroad to places new,
While in some bank my money grew,
Some people yes, tis aim they try,
Yet still a dream for you and I.

Late in life I thought again,
Together still through joys and pain,
Yes, we are wed through all those years
Sharing troubled times and tears,
Our money spent on all our plans,
Yet still so happy, holding hands,
Our children grown, as we grew old,
Your love for me worth more than gold
This love we share, I now caress,
I feel the secret of success.'

The Right Honourable The Lord Phillips of Worth Matravers

Lord Chief Justice of England and Wales

I do not believe that any Judge should ignore the following wise words of Portia in Act 4 of the *Merchant of Venice*.

'The quality of mercy is not strain'd;
It droppeth as the gentle rain from heaven
Upon the place beneath. It is twice blest:
It blesseth him that gives and him that takes.

'Tis mightiest in the mightiest; it becomes
The throned monarch better than his crown;
His sceptre shows the force of temporal power,
The attribute to awe and majesty,
Wherein doth sit the dread and fear of kings;

But mercy is above this sceptred sway,
It is enthroned in the hearts of kings,
And earthly power doth then show likest God's
When mercy seasons justice.'

Dame Fiona Reynolds, DBE

Director General, The National Trust

'Lines written a few miles above Tintern Abbey' (WORDSWORTH, 1798)

Therefore am I still
A lover of the meadows and the woods,
And mountains; and of all that we behold
From this green earth; of all the mighty world
Of eye and ear, both what they half-create,
And what perceive; well pleased to recognise
In nature and the language of the sense,
The anchor of my purest thoughts, the nurse,
The guide, the guardian of my heart, and soul
Of all my moral being.

Sir Cliff Richard, OBE

Singer, actor, businessman

—— INSPIRATIONAL BIBLE VERSE ——

'I can do everything through him (Christ) who gives me strength.'
(PHILIPPIANS 4:13)

Sir Jonathan Sacks, MA, PhD

Chief Rabbi of the United Hebrew Congregations of the Commonwealth

—— INSPIRATIONAL POEM ——

W. H. AUDEN, *from 'In Memory of W.B. Yeats'*

In the deserts of the heart
Let the healing fountain start,
In the prison of his days
Teach the free man how to praise.

4
Other Present-Day Insights

These insights and quotations were researched from a number of sources including the books set out in the Bibliography, the internet and the media. They provide ample scope for meditation and reflection.

Rebecca Adlington

Swimmer. Winner of two gold medals at the 2008 Olympics (400m and 800m freestyle). World record holder for 800m

'There is a tendency for some young people to think that they can get something for nothing these days. But you are never going to achieve anything unless you work hard. If you want your 15 minutes of fame, go on your reality TV show – that's fine. But if you want to achieve something that will last, something fantastic, put the work in. It will pay off. It is so satisfying that I achieved what I have myself. I haven't had sponsorship deals. I have had to train in a small, 25-metre pool without the best facilities and I haven't had money behind me. But I got there by working hard.'

'Whatever happens from now on [after winning second gold medal] will come second to my training. I will still be in the pool between 6am and 8am and between 5pm and 7pm. I will still be swimming 70,000 metres a week. You have to push yourself every single session. There are times when you don't even want to drive home because it hurts so much.'

Henry Allingham (born 6 June 1896)

At 112 year of age, Europe's oldest man

—— FORMULAE FOR LONGEVITY ——

1. 'I don't think there's a particular reason. The only thing I can say is all my life I have lived within my limitations, take life slowly, don't get any stress or strains. The more birthdays I enjoy, the longer I live.'

2. (jokingly) 'Cigarettes, whisky and wild women!'

Baroness Valerie Amos, PC

Politician and former Leader of the House of Lords

'My advice to women is to know what you want to achieve. Understand you need help and support and learn from your mistakes, have fun and be flexible. I think it is really important not to box yourself in and say, 'I am on this particular career path' because you lose opportunities that way. I think a lot of women constrain themselves because they look at their experiences and expertise in quite a narrow light. We need to be more open to opportunities and what we are prepared to think about. Women need to have more confidence in their experience and their skill. I've never been hung up thinking, "Can I actually do it?"'

Dame Julie Andrews, DBE

Emmy, Grammy, Bafta Golden Globe and Oscar award-winning actress and writer

'Success is terrifying. Like happiness, it is often appreciated in retrospect. It's only later that you place it in perspective. Years from now, I'll look back and say, "God, wasn't it wonderful?"'

Francesca Annis

Actress

On twin goals of success and happiness: 'It's an American import; really you just muddle through – like the Cavafy poem, *Ithaca*, you know: the journey of life is the thing, not the arriving.'

Lord Richard Attenborough, CBE

Film Director, actor. Winner of two Academy Awards, four BAFTA Awards and three Golden Globes.

'People have this image of me of being incredibly nice, but I'm not. I am ruthless. In terms of directing, I would move Heaven and Earth to get exactly what I wanted. That doesn't mean being dreadful to people or taking advantage. But there has been a certain single-mindedness in doing whatever it takes to get things the way I want them.'

Kenneth Baker, Baron Baker of Dorking, CH, PC

Politician

'Socialists make the mistake of confusing individual worth with success. They believe you cannot allow people to succeed in case those who fail feel worthless.'

Julianah Balogun-Oke

Single parent who lives on a sink estate who, on her own, brought up quadruplets who have all secured university places.

'It is the success of the quads that has got everyone asking how I've pulled off this apparent miracle (the statistics say that my children who grew up without a father present in their daily lives should be academic failures). Well, it is not rocket science. Simply put, it has always been my philosophy that it's not where you live but how you live – and that children learn by example. I've always known that education and hard work were the ways to improve my life, and I have instilled the same principles in my children.'

Julian Barratt and Noel Fielding (The Mighty Boosh)

Comedians and actors

—— TEN SECRETS OF SUCCESS ——

1. Don't know your place.

2. Keep your feet on the ground…

3. … but not too firmly on the ground.

4. Live in a dream world.

5. Look like amateurs.

6. Ignore outsiders.

7. Find a friend.

8. Keep it in the family.

9. Don't fall for fame.

10. Never network.

Dame Shirley Bassey, DBE

Singer, awarded the Legion d'honneur (1999), Most successful British solo artist of all time (Guinness Book of Records, 2000)

'I have found happiness in my work but not in my private life. The one takes from the other. I had to take from my private life to make my public life successful. I had to make a lot of sacrifices.'

David Beckham, OBE

Professional footballer

'Looking after your mates: it's an attitude I knew well enough from United. It's an attitude you'll see in every team that wins games and trophies.'

Tony Benn

Politician, former MP, Secretary of State for Industry and Minister of Technology. Diarist. Writer. Former RAF pilot.

'I realised the success of my first solo [flight] was entirely due to the fine instruction I had received; it was a tribute to that instruction that I never felt nervous once, and all the time had imagined what my instructor would be saying, so used had I got to doing everything with him behind me.'

'The only way to achieve anything is to get out there and do something, otherwise you will just sit at home and mope. As soon as you take action, you realise that you are not alone. Progress is a slow process. It is easy to feel that there is no point, but you have to remember that change does take a bit of time.'

'All progress comes from underneath. All real achievements are collective.'

'Five questions which should be asked of any powerful person:

1. What power have you got?

2. Where did you get it from?

3. In whose interests do you use it?

4. To whom are you accountable?

5. How do we get rid of you?'

Sir Tim Berners Lee, OM, KBE, FRS, FREng, FRSA

Computer scientist and inventor of the world wide web.
Holder of the 3Com Founders Chair at the MIT Computer Science and
Artificial Intelligence Laboratory

'I don't mind being, in the public context, referred to as the inventor of the World Wide Web. What I like is that image to be separate from private life, because celebrity damages private life.'

'I happened to come along with time, and the right interest and inclination, after hypertext and the Internet had come of age. The task left to me was to marry them together.'

'HTML started simply, with structured markup, no licensing requirements, and the ability to link to anything. More than anything, this simplicity and openness has led to its tremendous and continued success.'

'I know I'll have been successful when people are doing things with the Semantic Web that I can't imagine yet.'

Lord Karan Bilimoria, ACA, CBE, DL

*Businessman. Founder and Chairman of Cobra Beer,
Chancellor of Thames Valley University*

'All leaders need a strong sense of principles and values, but they must also be able to delegate, and the real secret to success is to employ people better than yourself and to trust and respect them. I'm reasonably good at production, sales, marketing and finance, but my directors are way better than me. I make them work together, know where we need to get to together and take them with me.'

Tony Blair

Politician. Prime Minister of the UK, 1997–2007

The secret of Tony Blair's success at the dispatch box: 'A pair of brogues. I know it's ridiculous, but I've worn them for every Prime Minister's Questions. I've actually had them for 18 years.'

—— WHAT MAKES A CHAMPION ——

'Champions need self-discipline to focus on a goal and lay aside other pleasures. They need to be motivated by a compassion for humanity.

They must be able to live with failure as well as success. And genuine champions are those who dare to create and innovate; creative people challenge the parameters. Above all, a champion requires courage; the courage lies not in acting without fear but acting despite fear.'

James Bradley

Poet

'Success'
'If success is a measure
Of how many nothings
Glorify my bank statements,
Then I am a failure,
After a score of
Meandering years.

If success is a measure
Of how many times
Your airbrushed face
Graces the screens
Then I am a failure

If success is knowing
Then I am a failure.

If success is peace,
Then I am a King.'

Kenneth Branagh

Actor, director

'My definition of success is control.'

'Because of the relative impact of what I was doing, because of that ubiquity, I suppose people thought there must be some sort of plan. What there was, above all was an extraordinary amount of energy. Without that energy one might have done things differently. Of course, one didn't just walk into things that were in front of one. What might be consistent between then and now is being passionate and energised about the things one loves.'

'The prestige of celebrity for its own sake is not something that interests me.'

Sir Richard Branson

Chairman of Virgin Group

'But becoming rich isn't just about piling up the money. Far from it. To be successful these days, you need to be rich in happiness, friendships, health and ideas.'

'What gets me up in the morning is the idea of making a difference. My definition of success in business has nothing to do with profits solely for their own sake. Success for me is whether you have created something you can be really proud of. Profits are necessary to invest in the next project – and pay the bills, repay investors and reward all the hard work – but that's all.'

Ken Bruce

Broadcaster (principally BBC Radio 2)

'I have had to prove that my success is not just based on my good looks.'

Darcey Bussell, CBE

Ballerina (retired)

'I always want to be the best. I push myself very hard. I practise for at least three hours, six days a week. I want every performance to be better than the last one.'

Sir Michael Caine, CBE

Actor

'When you reach the top, that's when the climb begins.'

Joe Calzaghe, CBE

WBO, WBC, WBA, Super Middleweight World Boxing Champion,
BBC Sports Personality of the Year 2007

'I know that if I am not at my best and I do not perform, I will lose. I'm never over-confident. Over-confidence is a weakness because it stops you training as hard as you should… Complacency beats fighters.'

Charlotte Church

Singer and television presenter

—— TIP 1 ——

'Try to be flexible and remain open to new opportunities. If life throws something unexpected at you, take it on the chin and roll with it. Who knows where it may lead.'

—— TIP 2 ——

'Take your own path in life. Don't let other people dictate the way.'

—— TIP 3 ——

'Your first ambition should be to be the best at what you do. If fame happens, it happens. If it's only fame you're interested in, let me tell you right now, you're going to be disappointed.'

Jeremy Clarkson

Television presenter, writer and journalist

'You should never have ambitions, because you either achieve them, in which case so what; or you don't in which case you have a life of disappointment.'

Dame Judi Dench, CH, DBE, FRSA

Award winning actress: nine BAFTAs, six Laurence Olivier Awards, two Screen Actors Guild Awards, an Academy Award, a Golden Globe and a Tony

'The more I do, the more frightened I get. But that is essential. Otherwise why would I go on doing it?'

'If you're taken up too much with being famous and doing things like having to wear really expensive clothes and things, you don't get enough time to actually think about what you're doing. I have no time for fame with nothing behind it.'

'I think you've got to have your feet planted firmly on the ground, especially in this business, and you must not believe things that are said or written about you, because everything gets out of proportion one way or the other.'

Sir James Dyson

Industrial designer

'Never ever give up; make it clear what you are doing and why you are doing it, publicly and internally; sometimes you cannot make a big leap but only lots of little improvements. In the end it adds up to a big improvement.'

Joe Elliot

Lead vocalist, Def Leppard, rock band

'A music career is like a wheel. As long as it keeps moving, the bit that's got "success" written on it ends up back at the top. You hope.'

Chris Eubank

Boxer who held the WBO Middleweight and Super Middleweight titles.
He was undefeated as a middleweight.

'All the rudiments of success in life can be found in ironing a pair of trousers.'

Sir Alex Ferguson, CBE

Football manager and former football player

'You have to then look ahead to see what you can be in two or three years' time and that is the hard part at this club [Manchester United] because as you do that you have still got to be successful. The hard thing is to change, to evolve the team and still be successful while having an eye for the future.'

'Winning and losing are twins and you have to deal with them in the right way. If you win, you don't need to gloat and, if you lose, you don't need to go bananas about it. You have to accept defeat – we all suffer them.'

Ralph Fiennes

Actor

'I call people "successful" not because they have money or their business is doing well but because, as human beings, they have a fully developed sense of being alive and are engaged in a lifetime task of collaboration with other human beings – their mothers and fathers, their family, their friends, their loved ones, the friends who are dying, the friends who are being born. Success? Don't you know it is all about being able to extend love to people? Really. Not in a big, capital-letter sense but in the everyday. Little by little, task by task, gesture by gesture, word by word.'

Sir David Frost, OBE

Television presenter and satirist

'Don't aim for success if you want it; just do what you love and believe in, and it will come naturally.'

Stephen Fry

Humourist, writer, actor, novelist, filmmaker and television presenter

'Much of success in life comes from being able to put yourself in the shoes of another: in the shoes of a prince or a pauper, a dictator or a dick-head, a burgomaster or a burger-flipper, regardless of degree, status or esteem; it's what imagination means.'

Ricky Gervais and Stephen Merchant

Comedians, writers, directors, actors

'If at first you don't succeed, remove all evidence you ever tried.' (DAVID BRENT, *The Office*)

Dame Jane Goodall, DBE

Primatologist, ethologist, and anthropologist. Founder of the Jane Goodall Institute. A United Nations Messenger of Peace. Awarded the Tyler Prize for Environmental Achievement, the French Legion d'Honneur, the Medal of Tanzania, Japan's prestigious Kyoto Prize, the Benjamin Franklin Medal in Life Science, the Gandhi-King Award for Nonviolence and the Spanish Premio Príncipe de Asturias.

'People say to me so often, "Jane, how can you be so peaceful when everywhere around you people want books signed, people are asking these questions and yet you seem peaceful?" and I always answer that it is the peace of the forest that I carry inside.'

'As a small child in England, I had this dream of going to Africa. We didn't have any money and I was a girl, so everyone except my mother laughed at it. When I left school, there was no money for me to go to university, so I went to secretarial college and got a job … If you really want something, and really work hard, and take advantage of opportunities, and never give up, you will find a way.'

Baroness Susan Greenfield, CBE

Professor of Synaptic Pharmacology at Lincoln College, Oxford, and Director of the Royal Institution, awarded the French Legion d'honneur

'A long time ago, I read an article on high-flying women (not specifically scientists) who suffer from the "impostor" syndrome. When I have spoken of this to other women, they have immediately owned up to feeling exactly the symptoms of this malady, namely a sneaky feeling that one day you will be caught out, that someone could do the job better – even your juniors – and that really it was just a fluke that you had arrived in your position. I wonder how many men actually feel that.'

Lewis Hamilton

Formula One racing driver

'I'm very, very competitive. I want to be the best at everything I do. It's not driving – it's everything – it might be playing my guitar, I try to be the best at it as I possibly can.'

'It's not about becoming rich and famous and squandering all your money. It's about enjoying life, working hard … dedication. … I would do this job for free.'

'The worst thing about it is losing your privacy. I am trying to deal with it at the moment, but I don't know the best way to do it. I am just trying to keep my head down, keep myself to myself and don't do anything lairy.'

Robert Harris

Best selling novelist. Former BBC TV reporter and journalist.

'People who succeed in life are rarely reflective. Their gaze is always on the future: that's why they succeed. It's not in their nature to remember what they were feeling, or wearing, or who was with them, or the scent of freshly cut grass in the churchyard on the day they were married, or the tightness with which their first baby squeezed their finger.'

Professor Stephen Hawking, CH, CBE, FRS, FRSA

Applied mathematician and theoretical physicist. Lucasian Professor of Mathematics at the University of Cambridge, and a Fellow of Gonville and Caius College, Cambridge.

'The victim should have the right to end his life, if he wants. But I think it would be a great mistake. However bad life may seem, there is always something you can do, and succeed at. While there's life, there is hope.'

'The downside of my celebrity is that I cannot go anywhere in the world without being recognised. It is not enough for me to wear dark sunglasses and a wig. The wheelchair gives me away.'

'I have had motor neurone disease for practically all my adult life. Yet it has not prevented me from having a very attractive family, and being successful in my work. This is thanks to the help I have received from Jane, my children, and a large number of other people and organisations. I have been lucky that my condition has progressed more slowly than is often the case. But it shows that one need not lose hope.'

Barry Hearn

Sports entrepreneur

'If you do anything just for the money, you don't succeed.'

Lenny Henry, CBE

Writer, comedian and actor. Winner, Golden Rose Award at the Montreux Television Festival. Trustee, Comic Relief. Opened the Lenny Henry Sickle Cell Clinic at King's College Hospital in London.

'I'm doing [2008] an MA at London University Royal Holloway in screenwriting for television and film. I had a production company and I was reading some scripts giving these really long-winded notes. I've worked with lots of writers and there is a shorthand that people have where you can learn to develop a script without necessarily having to go through the whole collegiate process. But I've always liked challenging myself and I've always liked this idea of not just giving up.

It's great being a comedian and an actor and a writer, but it's also good to sharpen resources, look back and figure out where I am from. Am I good enough for this? Is there something I can do to get better? And I saw this screenwriters' course and thought this is a great thing to do.'

Nicola Horlick

CEO Bramdean Asset Management

'What attributes make a successful business person? You need determination, enthusiasm and stamina. Be decisive and persuasive.'

'Maybe the answer is you can't necessarily have a happy marriage if you end up being a very high-powered woman. It may well be that men find it difficult living with a woman who's forging ahead and asserting her position.'

'A successful company is one with a strong culture and very little by way of office politics; an outwards facing business that is focussed on achieving the best for its clients. If you have the best quality people, which is crucial, you will succeed and this will be reflected in the profitability of the company.'

Chris Hoy, MBE

Track cyclist. Multiple Olympic Gold medal winner, 1 in 2004, 3 at Beijing Olympics, 8 Gold medals at World Championships (in 2002, 2004, 2005, 2006, 2007, 2008), 2 Gold medals at Commonwealth Games (2002 and 2006).

'I would have laughed if you'd told me even two years ago that I'd win three golds here [Beijing]. It's only in the last two or three years that we've real sprint coaches to guide us and give us the technical know how. I've always had the power, the speed, but it's about converting that speed, the timing of knowing when to use that speed. In the past, I didn't have a clue what I was doing. I would make mistakes but not learn from them whereas now if I make a mistake, we look at the video and the coaches say "Right do this, do that."'

Paul Ince

Manager of Blackburn Rovers FC, Former Football League manager, Premiership and England International footballer.

'The loneliness will never go away [he says of management]. That loneliness can be in victory or in defeat. Even when we won at Wembley, I didn't really get that buzz. It was great to see the players win something but it was only when I got home and sat on my own that I could reflect on what they'd achieved. So even in victory you're still lonely. The players are out on the town, dancing and drinking, but for me it's just about getting away to take stock and think.

General Sir Mike Jackson, GCB, CBE, DSO, DL

Former Chief of the General Staff

'Throughout my career, I have been taught, and I have striven to instill, the message that it is the soldiers themselves who will make the endeavour to succeed. As implied by the Sandhurst motto "Serve to Lead", one's loyalty must be from the bottom up.'

Sir Mick Jagger

Lead singer, 'Rolling Stones' rock group

'For most people, the fantasy is driving around in a big car, having all the chicks you want and being able to pay for it. It always has been, still is, and always will be. And anyone who says it isn't is talking bulls***.'

Sir Elton John, CBE

Rock/pop singer, composer, musician. Founder Elton John Aids Foundation.
Oscar for Best Original Song, 5 Grammy Awards.

'I cannot bear successful people who are miserable.'

'The great thing about rock and roll is that someone like me can be a star.'

'The whole point of being in this business and being blessed and being successful is that you're able to do things for your friends or your family, which means that they can have something special in their lives, too.'

Sir Tom Jones, OBE

Pop music singer

Reason for success: 'I think it's about ability too. And to get with the right producer, to have new ideas rather than to fall into a rut where you're doing everything the same. New ideas, fresh ideas that you need to embrace if you want something to sound new. There's a lot of different things that need to come together and I think I'm able to do that. I am open-minded enough to do it.'

Allan Leighton

Businessman, Chairman of Royal Mail

'In the end it is just about being focussed, listening, learning, having fun and, of course, it is also about good, old-fashioned common sense.'

Annie Lennox

Musician, vocalist, Academy Award-winning songwriter, charity campaigner

'When you're that successful, things have a momentum, and at a certain point you can't really tell whether you have created the momentum or it's creating you.'

'Ask yourself: Have you been kind today? Make kindness your daily modus operandi and change your world.'

Doris Lessing, CH, OBE

Writer, Nobel Prize Winner (Literature 2007)

'Some people obtain fame, others deserve it.'

'Any human anywhere will blossom in a hundred unexpected talents and capacities simply by being given the opportunity to do so.'

Leona Lewis

Pop and R&B singer-songwriter, winner of the UK television talent show
The X Factor

'I'm not a loud, extravagant person; I'm never going to be that and, to be honest, I don't want to be like that. I don't show off or boast, and it's pointless to think I'm going to be any different – I can't fake who I am – I have all these amazing people around who want to support me, and sometimes I feel I should act more confidently. But everyone around me says not to change anything, and Simon [Cowell] has always told me to be myself.'

'I don't drink alcohol, I've never done drugs and I'm not the type of person to come stumbling out of nightclubs. You never know what's true about celebrities, but I do know I'll be in trouble with my dad if I get up to anything like that. And I won't even do naked, half-naked or underwear shoots. All I want to do is my music, and just hearing my single on the radio the other day brought a tear to my eye; I was so happy.'

'I feel, and I hope, I'm the same girl I've always been and that my situation has changed, but I haven't.'

Sir Moir Lockhead, OBE

Chief Executive and Deputy Chairman First Group plc

'The one constant that all leaders and managers have to deal with is change. It is by equipping our managers to lead our people and change our companies as they make changes to meet new challenges that we can succeed … Most successful organisations develop a culture that welcomes change and the opportunities it brings.'

Dame Ellen MacArthur, DBE

Yachtswoman, holder of world record for fastest solo circumnavigation of the globe in a yacht, awarded the French Legion d'Honneur, founder of the Ellen MacArthur Trust

'Dogged determination is my greatest strength. I don't give up, I won't let go, in other aspects of my life as well as sailing.'

Colin Marshall, Baron Marshall of Knightsbridge

Businessman, former CEO and Chairman of British Airways,
Member of the House of Lords

'Formula for [British Airways corporate] success = evangelistic determination to strive for customer excellence.'

Sir Paul McCartney

Singer-songwriter, animal-rights activist, founder member of 'The Beatles'

'When you first get money, you buy all these things so no one thinks you're mean, and you spread it around. You get a chauffeur and you find yourself thrown around the back of this car and you think, I was happier when I had my own little car! I could drive myself!'

Sir Trevor McDonald, OBE

Journalist and television presenter

'I am a West Indian peasant who has drifted into this business and who has survived. If I knew the secret I would bottle it and sell it.'

Paul McKenna, PhD

Best selling author, hypnotist, television presenter

'*I'll back you*. Ultimately, all success in business comes down to getting other people to say those same three words to you in relation to your business, service or product … But people will only back you if you first do three things:

1. Let them know who you are;

2. Tell them the story of what you are offering;

3. Convince them it's worth having.'

Paul Merton

Actor, comedian, writer

'I enjoy the times I am not working as much as I enjoy the work. And it's nice to be a little bit exclusive. I think the best measure of success is that you don't have to work all the time.'

Sir John Mortimer, CBE, QC

Barrister, dramatist and author

'Being successful in England is a dangerous occupation.'

Kate Moss

Model

'People think your success is just a matter of having a pretty face. But it's easy to be chewed up and spat out. You've got to stay ahead of the game to be able to stay in it.'

Theo Paphitis

Entrepreneur, Chairman of Ryman, 'Dragon' in BBC TV programme 'Dragon's Den'

'Fear is an essential ingredient in every successful business. If you have no fear you will come a cropper since only fools rush in. Every top-class sportsman and woman has a built-in fear of failure. That's what makes them so damn good and so damn hard to beat. And it's no different in business.' (*Enter the Dragon*, Orion, 2008)

'There are three reasons to be in business: to make money, to have fun, and to make money.'

Cecilia Parkin

Poet

'Success'
'How do you measure life's success
How do you see it my friend?
The high powered job—and with it esteem,
The gloss and the glitter, the trappings well seen.
Select company to keep, the right places to meet.
Is that how you measure Success!.'

'Not so' said our Lord, 'That's not what I see
My measure's in a different way.
It's all there in the commandments I ask you to keep
As you live out your life every day.

It's in the clasp of the hand from someone you've helped,
A 'Hello' from a once unfriendly face,
It's taking a road you don't want to walk—
Knowing what it will embrace.

It's the cheerful and thankful, who make light of their cares
And look out for others in need.
It's giving your all, with no thought of reward
Through all the laughter and tears.

No public acclaim, no exhortation to fame
Is ever likely to reach your ears,
But as you lay down your head, the day's life well led,
THAT IS SUCCESS, my friend'.

Nina Pell

'The Times' National Su Doku Champion 2008

'Secret of my success: logic, guesswork – and speed.'

Trevor Phillips, OBE

Chair of the Equality and Human Rights Commission, board member of the Almeida Theatre in Islington, Aldeburgh Productions and the Bernie Grant Centre in Tottenham. Patron of the Sickle Cell Society.

'Isaiah Berlin was adamant that the success of a pluralist society is not about ignoring the identities that are important to people, but about fitting people together, so there is a mutually beneficial cultural exchange. Can faith help us to achieve that exchange? Yes, I think it can. Faith is no longer a private matter. Faith communities provide support with good governance, tackling deprivation, housing, regeneration, empowering communities and improving the local environment.'

Kevin Pietersen

Cricketer, Captain of the England Cricket Team

'I am not bound by material things. It's being successful that drives me forward. I love success. I don't wake up in the morning thinking: "Great – I've got one million pounds in the bank". I wake up happy because I am a successful part of a successful team. It's that success that brings all the media coverage, the first-night parties, the endorsements. I will never lose sight of that. It has come very quickly – sooner than even I expected. But it's great to know that if I continue in the same vein, then I can do exactly what I want with the rest of my life. I will be financially secure.'

Courtney Pine, OBE

Jazz musician

'The reason for my success is perseverance and the attitude that I won't give up. If I was in any other business, I'd have been closed down by now. I was nearly bankrupt. What I'm doing is unique and I get an audience every night.'

Philip Pullman

Prize winning, best selling author

'I have always written what I wanted to write, I have never considered the audience for one second. Ever. It's none of their business what I write! Before publication, I am a despot … I was saying that, feeling that, working like that, 30 years ago, when I wasn't successful.'

Paula Radcliffe, MBE

Long distance runner. Winner of World Championship, Marathon, Commonwealth Games 5,000 metres, European Championship 1,000m, 3 World Cross Country Championships, 6 City Marathons. BBC Sports Personality of the Year, 2002.

'I do think that sometimes you have to go through setbacks to get what you really want. Look at the number of times I was pipped at the post in the world cross-country before I actually won it. Just because things haven't gone right in the past, doesn't mean that you can't go back and try even harder the next time.'

Gordon Ramsay, OBE

Chef, television personality, entrepreneur

'If it is success you are after, it helps if you are a worker. I know there are people out there, highly successful people, who seem to have achieved great things with minimum effort, but I haven't a clue how they do that. I need to work hard and I need to be seen by my staff. That way everyone knows how high the bar is set. This in itself creates a bond with your staff, and without them, you have nothing. In a successful business, you need their respect and their loyalty. Achieve that, and you are well and truly on your way to success.'

Vanessa Redgrave, CBE

Actress and social activist

'Integrity is so perishable in the summer months of success.'

Nick Reed

Playwright

'Personal development sandwich, *The BLT*: "Believe in yourself", "Let go of the past", "Take responsibility for the future".' (COLIN in the play, *Lifecoach*)

Dame Diana Rigg, DBE

Actress

—— ON SUCCESS ——

'I should have handled it better. Had more fun. Not naughty fun. But just, you know, I sometimes think, when I look back on those days: why didn't I have more confidence? Why didn't I know I was pretty good-looking? It is probably to do with my Yorkshire upbringing. Always thinking that people might be saying, "Who does she think she is?"'

Andrew Roberts

Historian, writer, journalist

'Confidence of success is almost success, and obstacles often fall by themselves before a determination to overcome.' (*Salisbury: Victorian Titan, 1999*)

J.K. Rowling, OBE

Author, Philanthropist, Trustee of Comic Relief, President of One Parent Families

'We do not need magic to change the world; we carry all the power we need inside ourselves already: we have the power to imagine better.'

'I think you have a moral responsibility, when you've been given far more than you need, to do wise things with it and give intelligently.'

June Sarpong, MBE

TV personality, charity worker, businesswoman

'Women are under huge pressure, much more now than women of, say, my grandmother's generation. It was easier to meet someone, now it's hard to meet a man who is not intimidated by a successful woman. You're made to feel bad if you don't work in order to have children – and on top of all that you're expected to look like a supermodel! … Because I work in the media, I know what an illusion it all is.'

Vidal Sassoon

Hairdresser and businessman

'The only place where success comes before work is in a dictionary.'

Baroness Scotland of Asthal, PC, QC

Barrister and the current Attorney General for England and Wales

'Both my parents always said everyone is the artifice of their own good fortune and they made it absolutely clear that every single one of us has been given a gift and it is our job basically to take that gift, hone it and then use it for the benefit of other people. That was drummed into you as what you had to do and there was no point in saying you didn't have a talent because that was to deny what God had given you.'

Eleanor Simmonds

13-year-old winner of two gold medals for swimming, at the 2008 Paralympics

'It's hard work. On a training day I'm up at 5.15am for swimming at 6am. After school I'm back at the pool for more training. But it's what you do if you want to go to the Olympics.'

Anna Sofat, MBA

Founder of the women's wealth management company Addidi.

'Successful women need to succeed – it's rarely about the money, it's about wanting to prove something to themselves or to someone else. Once they reach a certain level they think, "Right, I've set out to do that and I have achieved that." But they then don't think, "Now I want to be CEO." They think, "What else is there in life? Is this what I really want?" … corporate life and culture as it is today is no longer appealing to women, and certainly not to women with families.'

Sir Jackie Stewart, OBE

Former racing driver, winner of three Formula 1 World Driver's Championships, Commentator

'If winning is not enough, what is enough? In my view, "enough" is winning over an extended period of time in a variety of different fields and, the key to achieving long-term success lies in nurturing meaningful, long-term relationships.'

Sir Tom Stoppard, CBE

Playwright and screenwriter

'The trouble with success is that it immediately diminishes your mental conception of what it should be.'

Sir Alan Sugar

Businessman and broadcaster

'Formula for success – it's having the right stuff in the right place at the right time, and neither too much nor too little of it.'

Gordon Sumner, CBE (aka 'Sting')

Musician, songwriter, director, actor

'Success always necessitates a degree of ruthlessness. Given the choice of friendship or success, I'd probably choose success. We're not in control of the forces that could make us next week's has-beens.'

Dame Elizabeth Taylor, DBE

Actress (two-time Academy winner), AIDS charity campaigner

'Success is a great deodorant. It takes away all your past smells.'

'It's all about hope, kindness and a connection with one another.'

Lady Margaret Thatcher, LG, OM, PC, FRS

Prime Minister of the United Kingdom from 1979 to 1990
and Leader of the Conservative Party from 1975 to 1990

'What is success? I think it is a mixture of having a flair for the thing that you are doing; knowing that it is not enough; that you have got to have hard work and a certain sense of purpose.'

'One only gets to the top rung of the ladder by steadily climbing up one at a time, and suddenly all sorts of powers, all sorts of abilities which you thought never belonged to you – suddenly become within your own possibility and you think, "Well, I'll have a go, too".'

'Success is having a flair for the thing you are doing.'

Daley Thompson, CBE

Former decathlete. Winner of Olympic gold medals for the decathlon in 1980 and 1984. Broke the world record for the event 4 times. Gold medal winner at the Commonwealth European and World Championships.

'If you're not in it, you can't win it.'

'Achieving success on the track is not a sole effort – it requires team effort.'

Alan Titchmarsh, MBE, DL

Broadcaster, celebrity gardener

'Success genuinely surprises me. Where fiction is concerned, I still have the feeling that I've been allowed to play with the grown-ups.'

Russell Watson

Tenor

'Being surrounded by other celebrities telling me how wonderful I am is not my idea of fun.'

'Being close to death has taught me that life is a great gift – maybe I didn't appreciate that fully until I nearly lost it. The important things in life are not my voice and selling records, but my children's love and friendships. I'm incredibly grateful that I'm still here.'

Fay Weldon, CBE

Novelist, playwright and essayist

'People give us credit only for what we ourselves believe.'

'If everybody likes something, you've failed. Consensus is not what you're after.'

'Fame is a very odd word which doesn't really seem to apply, only in that you get the vague thought you shouldn't go out with your tights laddered.'

'As a kind of bonus, you found you could do this thing, you could write, and it was much easier than you ever thought and there was an exhilaration. And then a whole set of other problems were created. So you haven't lost your problems, but they are not as basic as where and how are you going to live? You are lifted up. But you don't forget.'

Katherine Whitehorn

Journalist and writer

'Out of every fruition of success, no matter what, comes forth something to make a new effort necessary.'

Dr. Rowan Williams

Archbishop of Canterbury

'"Launch out into the deep": understand that your life lies in the not knowing as well as the knowing; that your life lies in understanding your limits; that your life lies in a letting-go which allows love, reconciliation and promise and which, if you believe it, aligns you with precisely that energy of creative gift which sustains the entire universe.'

Victoria Wood, CBE

BAFTA award-winning comedian, actor, singer and writer

'I once won a poll of People You'd Most Like to Live Next-Door To. That gave them a laugh at home, I can tell you. The Queen Mother came second to me. I should imagine she was very annoyed about that.'

'I've got so many other things I want to do. I just feel another direction looming. I would really like to write some films. I've got things in me that can't necessarily be encapsulated in a stand-up show. You can only follow your instincts and I don't want to drop back down and end up doing little theatres. I'm having a ball, but nobody stays at the top. Very, very few people can keep it going.'

Benjamin Zephaniah

Poet. Social campaigner

'Writers and artists who see themselves as working outside the establishment are constantly being accused of selling out as soon as they have any kind of success. I've been called a sell-out for selling too many books, for writing books for children, for performing at the Royal Albert Hall, for going on Desert Island Discs, and for appearing on the Parkinson show. But I want to reach as many people as possible without compromising the content of my work.'

5
Success Formulae and Traits of Historic Britons

The following 10 historic figures were selected from *100 Greatest Britons*, the BBC survey undertaken in 2002 and voted on by 1 million members of the public. The success traits that are outlined have been deduced from the biographies of the individuals.

Isambard Kingdom Brunel, FRS (1806–1859)

Engineer

—— SUCCESS FORMULA TRAITS ——

Agent of change, ruthless and clinical in methods, organisational skill, originality and boldness of thought, ceaseless toil.

—— INSIGHTS ——

These formula attributes were drawn from Steven Brindle's book *Brunel, The Man Who Built the World*. Brindle reviewed Brunel's office diaries for the 1840s and 1850s which give a fascinating insight into 'ceaseless toil', showing how it transcended mere hard work. The diaries 'reveal an almost unbelievable daily schedule with Brunel travelling, inspecting works and attending meetings from 6 or 7 in the morning until late in the evening day after day.' Brindle gives further detail on this schedule with an insight on how it was maintained by quoting GT Clarke, an assistant of Brunel's:

> 'I never met his equal for sustained power of work. After a hard day spent in preparing and delivering evidence, he would attend consultations until a late hour; and then, secure against interruption, sit down to his papers, and draw specifications, write letters or reports, or make calculations all through the night. If at all pressed for time he slept in his armchair for two or three hours, and at early dawn he was ready for the work of the day. When he travelled he usually started about four or five in the morning, so as to reach his ground by daylight. ... This power of work was no doubt aided by the abstemiousness of his habits and by his light and joyous temperament. One luxury, tobacco, he indulged in to excess, and probably to his injury. At all times, even in bed, a cigar was in his mouth; and wherever he was engaged, there, near at hand, was the enormous leather cigar case so well known to his friends, and out of which he was quite as ready to supply their wants as his own.'

Another insight to Brunel is set out in R. Angus Buchanan's book, *Brunel, The Life and Times of Isambard Kingdom Brunel,* when he quoted William Hawes:

> 'The most striking feature of his character as a young man, and one which afterwards produced such great results, was an entire abnegation of self in his intercourse with his friends and associates. ... His influence among them was unbounded, but never sought by

him: it was the result of his love of fair play, of his uniform kindness and willingness to assist them, of the confidence he inspired in his judgement, and the simplicity and high mindedness of his character.'

—— QUOTE ——

'Nothing but *advantage* can *in the end* come from doing right.' (ISAMBARD KINGDOM BRUNEL)

Sir Winston Churchill, KG, OM, CH, TD, FRS, PC (1874–1965)

Politician, Prime Minister of United Kingdom 1940–45 and 1951–55.
Leader of Great Britain during World War 2. Writer and artist.

—— SUCCESS FORMULA TRAITS ——

Fearlessness, deep emotional capacity, robust enjoyment of life, stubborn refusal to compromise with the second-rate and single-minded devotion to duty.

—— INSIGHTS ——

These formula attributes were identified by Walter Graebner, a professional journalist who spent hundreds of hours with Churchill, in his book, *My Dear Mister Churchill*. Graebner further described him:

> 'He was English to the core with an old-fashioned, swashbuckling Elizabethan Englishness that expressed itself at all times grandly and without petty restraint. Therein, I think, lay much of the secret of his greatness and the power he had to capture the admiration and affection of the whole world. He was the epitome of all that was best in the English character.'

Graebner provides a fascinating insight into what many would think were Churchill's eccentric working habits:

> 'He remained in bed all morning as a rule. Only special circumstances, such as a Cabinet crisis, or a warm and sunny day at Chartwell, could induce him to rise before lunch. He liked having his feet up, and his mind worked well and quickly in bed. It was easy for him to stay in bed and work because near at hand was everything that anyone could want in an office. The big double bed provided plenty of space on both sides for papers, books, and so on. Work in actual progress was done on a short-legged mahogany tray about 30 × 18 inches which fitted snugly over his torso. For greater comfort the tray was fitted with a set of small rubber pads on which he could rest his elbows. Within easy reach of his bed, whether at Chartwell, Hyde Park Gate or 10 Downing Street, stood a narrow table with two telephones – a direct line to his secretaries' office downstairs, and an outside connection…'

'All the great things are simple and many can be expressed in a single word: freedom, justice, honour, duty, mercy, hope.'

'Attitude is a little thing that makes a big difference.'

'Courage is rightly esteemed the first of human qualities … because it is the quality which guarantees all others. Continuous effort – not strength or intelligence – is the key to unlocking our potential. However beautiful the strategy, you should occasionally look at the results.'

'Success is going from failure to failure without loss of enthusiasm.'

'No one can guarantee success in war but only deserve it.'

Oliver Cromwell (1599–1658)

Military and political leader,
Lord Protector of England, Scotland and Ireland (1653–1658)

—— FORMULA TRAITS FOR MILITARY SUCCESS ——

'He learned fast; he was energetic; he had a good eye for ground; he had both physical and moral coverage; he was a good operational and logistic planner; he was bold and innovative … perhaps above all he was a great trainer.'

—— INSIGHTS ——

These traits for military success featured in *Old Ironsides, The Military Biography of Oliver Cromwell*, by Frank Kitson, who elaborated on Cromwell's 'personal' qualifications for command as follows:

> Knowledge of the job. 'At the start of the Civil War in 1642 the 43-year-old Cromwell had no military understanding of experience or of study. He was obliged to pick it up as he went along.' [He was a fast learner.];

> Communication skills. 'When it came to expressing himself militarily, in marked contrast to his political utterances, he was not only clear and accurate but also persuasive and sometimes inspiring';

> Energy and conviction [as commander] 'also needs vast amounts of physical energy … and he needs mental energy … Certainly Cromwell had the will for this … Cromwell was upheld by the feeling that he rode for God and that God would look after him … As a result he managed to keep going at a terrific rate for two or three months at a time … Cromwell was not ideally suited either physically or mentally to the operational command of an army, but by sheer force of character he managed to carry it through';

> Courage. 'Overall it is clear that Cromwell showed steady courage throughout his military career through many encounters with the enemy';

> Planning. 'Cromwell's strategic arrangements were particularly notable for the extent to which he foresaw his future requirements and for the way he set about obtaining the resources he needed';

Delegation. 'In battle Cromwell usually let his subordinate commanders get on with their appointed tasks without getting too closely involved himself. But he kept a close eye on events in order to commit his reserve at the right moment at the right place';

Involvement. 'Reaching the right conclusion [about military action] requires great strength of will and sound judgement, but he has not only to overcome the enemy but also to carry his own side with him. In the 17th century, commanders usually held a council of war before the start of each new phase of an operation in which they listened to the views of their subordinates … Cromwell always tried to get his council to back him, even going to the extent of getting someone else to put forward his view so that he could appear to be supporting them rather than putting up the idea himself. But once a decision was taken, he was very determined to see it through.

—— QUOTES ——
(all by Oliver Cromwell)

'Be please to reform the abuses of all professions: and if there be anyone that makes many poor to make a few rich, that suits not a Commonwealth.'

'He who stops being better stops being good.'

Charles Robert Darwin (1809–1882)

Naturalist, geologist, evolutionary biologist and author.
Originator of the concept of natural selection.

—— FORMULA TRAITS ——

Energy of body, energy of mind, studious, methodical, steadiness, great curiosity and love of the new and marvellous.

—— INSIGHTS ——

This formula is distilled from a survey undertaken in 1873, by Francis Galton who asked Darwin to list the special mental qualities that he felt he might possess. Darwin considered that 'all I have learnt of any value has been self taught' and stressed the quality of perseverance by often using the expression: 'It's dogged as does it' from Anthony Trollope's work *The Last Chronicle of Basset.* He responded to the survey questions as follows:

Politics? – Liberal or radical

Health? – good when young – bad for last 33 years

Temperament? – somewhat nervous

Energy of body? Energy shown by much activity, and whilst I had health, power of resisting fatigue. An early riser in the morning.

Energy of mind? – shown by rigorous and long-continued work on same subject, as 20 years on the *Origin of the Species* and 9 years on *Cirripedia.*

Memory? – Memory very bad for dates, and for learning by rote; but good in retaining a general or vague recollection of many facts

Studiousness? – Very studious, but not large acquirements

Independence of judgement? – I think fairly independent; but I can give no instances. I gave up common religious belief almost independently from my own reflections

Strongly marked mental peculiarities? – Steadiness, great curiosity about facts and their meaning. Some love of the new and marvellous

Special talents? – None, except for business, as evinced by keeping accounts, replies to correspondence, and investing money very well. Very methodical in all my habits.

Tim Lewens adds a moral dimension to this list in his book, *Darwin*, when he quotes Darwin: 'I have so lately endeavoured to shew that the social instincts – the prime principle of man's moral constitution –with the aid of active intellectual powers and the effects of habit, naturally lead to the golden rule, "As ye would that man should do to you, do ye to them likewise", and this lies at the foundation of morality.'

—— QUOTE ——

'I am the supreme judge of my own conduct, and in the words of Kant, I will not in my own person violate the dignity of humanity.' (Darwin)

Queen Elizabeth I (1533–1603)

Queen of England and Queen of Ireland 1558–1603

—— SUCCESS FORMULA TRAITS ——

Valour, spirit, prudence and 'marvellous good fortune'.

—— INSIGHTS ——

These characteristics were identified by Henry III of France according to Anne Somerset in her book *Elizabeth I*. In the same book, Somerset cites Francis Bacon as noting what today would be called people skills: 'one of the most judicious princes in discerning of spirits that ever governed' and 'proficient in the reading of men as well as books.' These skills were also evident in evoking the love of the people, as Somerset explains: 'the love she had lavished on her subjects had been reciprocated in full measure…'

Queen Elizabeth recognised the importance of communication in an age which lacked today's sophisticated media. One method she employed was to undertake a series of tours of the country or progresses where she came face to face with her people. Somerset explains: 'In the course of her reign she traversed across perhaps a third of her kingdom, covering an area which extended westwards to Bristol, southwards to Southampton, eastwards to Norwich, and with Chartley in Staffordshire at its northernmost point … she recognised that progresses served as an invaluable means of interaction between subject and sovereign. If she had led a more sedentary existence, the only contact which the Court vouchsafed to the vast majority of her people would have derived from their dealings with her purveyors, and she believed that they deserved to be introduced to a more positive side of royal government. Her tours were designed to let her reach as wide an audience as was possible in an age which lacked sophisticated means of mass communication, and she embarked on them with the deliberate intention of transforming the monarchy from a remote and faceless entity to a living presence.

The Queen's passage through town and countryside made an impressive spectacle … accompanied by a bagged train of between four hundred to six hundred carts, the Court would laboriously uproot itself to accompany her on her peregrinations … A French ambassador who witnessed one such ceremonial entry [into London] in 1579 was transported by the sight of her 'more beautiful than ever, bedizened like the sun, and mounted on a fine Spanish horse; and with so many people before her that it was a marvellous thing. They did not merely honour her, but they worshipped her, kneeling on the ground, with a thousand blessings and joyful remarks.'… The pace she travelled at was excruciatingly slow, for she regarded it as important to take time to acknowledge the plaudits of the crowds that gathered on the waysides to watch her go by. … She ordered her carriage to be taken sometimes where the crowd seemed thickest, and stood up and thanked the people [remarked even Guerau de Spes, a known critic of the Queen].

Always, the masses who turned out for her were delighted by the inimitable grace with which she accepted her homage, and by the trouble she took to show she did not take their affection for granted … she showed herself at both sides of her coach unto them, and, often times said, "I thank you, I thank you all."'

—— QUOTES ——

[It was the love of her people which made] 'a heavy burden light, and a kingdom's care but easy carriage to me.' (Queen Elizabeth I)

[On assuming the throne] 'She had been well instructed by experience and adversity, two excellent teachers.' (Neale)

Sir Alexander Fleming (1881–1955)

Microbiologist and pharmacologist. discovery of the enzyme lysozyme in 1922 and, along with Australian Howard Florey, discovery of the antibiotic substance penicillin from the fungus Penicillium notatum. Nobel prize winner.

—— FORMULA TRAITS ——

'An innate curiosity and perceptiveness regarding natural phenomena, insight into the heart of a problem, technical ingenuity, persistence in seeing a job through and that physical and mental toughness that is essential to a top-class investigator.' (LEONARD COLEBROOK, British medical researcher)

—— INSIGHTS ——

Despite these qualities for success identified by Colebrook, arguably without good fortune he would not have achieved his scientific breakthroughs. As the French writer Andre Maurois pointed out in his book, *Life of Alexander Fleming* (1961):

> 'Had he not been an untidy man and apt to leave his culture exposed on the laboratory table the spore of hyssop mould, the penicillin notatum, might never have floated in from Praed Street and settled on his dish of staphylocci.'

But Maurois went on:

> 'Yet had Fleming not possessed immense knowledge and an unremitting gift of observation he might not have observed the effect of the hyssop mould.' 'Fortune,' remarked Pasteur, 'favours the prepared mind.' (ANDRE MAUROIS, French writer, *Life of Alexander Fleming* 1961)

Kevin Brown, in his book, *Penicillin Man*, gives a further insight:

> 'his taciturnity, which made the inner man somewhat unfathomable, had some advantages in his dealings with the press as he was not tempted to make sweeping statements or indiscreet comments that could have hit the headlines.'

Fleming himself commented on this trait when he said: 'if I had been of a more talkative nature I would soon have found myself in trouble.' But, as Brown noted, Fleming took this approach a little far: 'a conversation with him was like playing tennis with a man who, when he received a service, put the ball in his pocket.' Brown further revealed: 'Fleming was equally comfortable with silence and could stand staring at someone without exchanging a word and without the slightest embarrassment or discomfort, making his conversations "masterpieces of brevity".'

A final, droll insight, again from Brown's book: 'The actress Marlene Dietrich had a crush on him, invited him to dinner and cast his horoscope, in return for which he put his hand in his pocket and presented her with one of his mould medallions.'

—— QUOTE ——

During a visit to Turin in 1946, he [Fleming] was greeted by the Communist mayor as a 'representative of the working man', to which he replied that 'he was a good workman and that was the only way to success'.

Vice Admiral Horatio Nelson, 1st Viscount Nelson, KB

British Admiral

—— SUCCESS FORMULA TRAITS ——

For military success, also known as 'The Nelson touch': logistical genius, truly care about the men under command, confidence which inspires others, daring, empowerment of captains to pursue overall battle plan with their own initiative, thinking outside the box.

'The Nelson touch' was a man management and leadership approach developed by Nelson, on a blend of discipline and sympathetic approach to his men that was based on mutual trust. It way a key differentiator with opposing naval commanders. In his book *Lord Nelson and His Way of War*, Joel Hayward defined 'The Nelson touch' further:

> 'Nelson, logistical genius. He worked tirelessly to supply his men with fresh food whenever possible and gather the materials needed to keep the ships in fighting order. At the Battle of Trafalgar, he had obsessive concern for the logistical train to support his 27-ship fleet;
>
> Nelson truly cared about the men under his command. Although he understood the need for and applied discipline, he was not bullying or cruel to his men who were often 'pressed' into service, i.e. virtually enslaved by press gangs;
>
> Nelson's own confidence inspired, by example, those under his command. By all accounts, the English sailors went into battle confident of victory, simply because Nelson was their leader;
>
> Nelson empowered his captains (he referred to his fellow officers as his "band of brothers"). He was very careful, often in lengthy informal meetings (sometimes over meals) to explain his overall plan for the battle but he left the details and implementation up to each captain. Thus, as the battle unfolded, the English always had the advantage of individual initiative, while the competing fleets tended to rely on direct orders issued through signal flags, flags which were often obscured by smoke from black powder gunfire or the interference of other ships;
>
> Thinking "outside the box". Nelson generally gained the advantage by doing the unexpected or taking what others would see as unacceptable risk as in the Battle of the Nile, which drove Napoleon

from North Africa, when he engaged in a night battle – a very chancy affair.'

The one caveat exposed by Hayward to Nelson's military genius is that it did not appear to be transferable to 'other fields of endeavour'. Hayward considered him an abysmally inept leader on land, impulsive, impatient and reckless when victory was possible. Hayward points out that both of Nelson's injuries (loss of vision in one eye and loss of an arm) occurred in land battles in which he had been tasked to overcome forts. He lost both battles.

—— QUOTES ——

'And, Sir, the secret of his victories?''By his unservicelike, forsaken ways, Sir. He made the whole fleet love him, damn his eyes!' (ROBERT GRAVES, 1805)

'I owe all my success in life to having been always a quarter of an hour before my time.' (HORATIO NELSON, 1758–1805, English admiral)

Sir Isaac Newton, FRS (1642–1727)

Professor of Mathematics at Cambridge University, Member of Parliament, Master of the Mint and President of the Royal Society

—— SUCCESS FORMULA TRAITS ——

Clarity of mind, vigour and regularity, inventiveness, thoroughness, preoccupation with systematic knowledge, single minded, supreme self confidence and 'of a very serious and compos'd frame of mind, yet I have often seen him laugh.'

These were some of the characteristics which contributed to Newton's success, gleaned from Peter Ackroyd's book, *Newton*. Of course, they do not totally explain his genius – this is something he was born with.

Ackroyd provides an example of Newton's single-mindedness when he quotes one of Newton's assistants: 'he always kept close to his studies, very rarely went a visiting, and had as few visitors.''I never knew him take any Recreation or Pastime, either in Riding out to take the Air, Walking, Bowling, or any other Exercise whatever, Thinking all Hours lost, that was not spent on his studies.' Ackroyd explains: 'Here is the portrait of a secluded if not precisely misanthropic scholar, a pale devotee of sometime secret sciences.' He is, in William Blake's phrase, 'the virgin shrouded in snow', in the tradition of other melancholy scholars such as Boyle and Evelyn.

In his book *Isaac Newton, The Last Sorcerer*, Michael White gives another example, this time of apparently foolhardy single-mindedness when he quotes Newton describing one of his experiments:

> 'I took a bodkin [from the illustration accompanying this entry in Newton's notebook, astonishingly, this appears to be a small dagger similar to an envelope knife], and put it between my eye and the bone as near to the backside of my eye as I could, and pressing my end with the end of it (so as to make the curvature in my eye) there appeared several white, dark and coloured circles. Which circles were plainest when I continued to rub my eye with the point of the bodkin, but if I held my eye with it yet the circles would grow faint often disappear until I resumed them by moving my eye or the bodkin.'

As White remarked,'by nearly causing permanent blindness he came close to destroying his scientific career almost before it had begun.'

'Truth is the offspring of silence and unbroken meditation'

'If I have ever made any valuable discoveries, it has been owing more to patient attention, than any other talent.'

'I keep the subject of my inquiry constantly before me, and wait till the first dawning opens gradually, by little and little, into a full and clear light.'

William Shakespeare (1564–1616)

Poet, playwright, actor

Intense and overwhelming energy, ambition, buoyancy, an inward easiness of spirit, vitality, preternatural alertness, gentleness (a gentleman), determination, compassion and sensitivity.

This formula (drawn from Peter Ackroyd's book, *Shakespeare the biography*, Vintage 2006), is a long and complicated one, as might be expected for the world's greatest ever playwright, and is probably as much about his character as his secrets of success.

Ackroyd also points to another key trait of Shakespeare – hard work.

> 'The run of a new play was 4–6 weeks and there were always revivals and reworkings. For Shakespeare, in addition to actually writing plays and in quick succession, there were rehearsals, playing in the afternoon and, in the evening, learning of lines. Shakespeare was therefore 'continually and exhaustingly occupied. JMW Turner once said that the secret of genius was "hard work", a sentiment with which Shakespeare would have agreed.'

But despite all of his attributes, luck just may have played its part in his success. Ackroyd quotes a lineal descendant of Joan Shakespeare, the poet's sister, 'that Shakespeare owed his rise in life, and his introduction to the theatre, to his accidentally holding the horse of a gentleman at the door of a theatre on his first arriving in London; his appearance led to enquiry and subsequent patronage.' Although this notion was repeated in the 18th century by Samuel Johnson, Ackroyd goes on to say that it was more likely that Shakespeare's opportunities came from his employment as an actor.

—— INSPIRATIONAL VERSES ——

(Shakespeare, *King Lear*)
'Have more than thou showest,
Speak less than thou knowest,
Lend less than thou owest,
Ride more than thou goest,
Learn more than thou trowest,

Set less than thou throwest;
Leave thy drink and thy whore,
And keep in-a-door,
And thou shalt have more
Than two tens to a score.'

(SHAKESPEARE, *Henry VI)*
Didst thou never hear,
That things ill got had ever bad success?

Field Marshal Arthur Wellesley,
1st Duke of Wellington, KG, KP, GCB, GCH, PC, FRS (1769–1852)

Soldier, defeated Napoleon at the Battle of Waterloo, statesman – twice Prime Minister of the United Kingdom

FORMULA TRAITS

Staunch, straightforward, plain speaking, moral and physical courage, deep sense of duty and honesty.

—— INSIGHTS ——

The above formula was interpreted from Charles Greville's epitaph which Christopher Hibbert quoted in his book, *Wellington, a Personal History*:

> 'Charles Greville, who had known and understood the Duke so well, and who had not hesitated in the past to specify his faults and foibles, provided a just and well-considered epitaph:
>
> > "He was beyond all doubt, a very great man – the only great man of the present time – and compatible, in point of greatness, to the most eminent of those who have lived before him. His greatness, was the result of a few striking qualities – a perfect simplicity of character without a particle of vanity or conceit but with a thorough and strenuous self-reliance, a severe truthfulness, never misled by fancy or exaggeration, and an ever-abiding sense of duty and obligation which made him the humblest of citizens and most obedient of subjects. The Crown never possessed a more faithful, devoted and disinterested subject. Without personal attachment to any of the Monarchs whom he served, and fully understanding and appreciating their individual merits and demerits, he alike reverenced their great office in the persons of each of them, and would at any time have sacrificed his ease, his fortune, or his life, to serve the Sovereign and the State. He was treated with greater respect than any individual not of Royal birth, and the whole Royal Family admitted him to a peculiar and exclusive familiarity and intimacy in their intercourse with him, which, while he took it in the easiest manner, and as if naturally due to him, he never abused or presumed upon. No man was more respectful or deferential towards the Sovereign and other Royal personages, but at the same time he always gave them his opinions and counsels with perfect

frankness and sincerity, and never condescended to modify them to suit their prejudices or wishes. Upon every occasion of difficulty, public or private, he was always appealed to, and he was always ready to come forward and give his assistance in his characteristic plain, and straightforward manner. He had all his life long been accustomed to be consulted, and he certainly liked it to the last, and was pleased with the marks of deference and attention which were continually paid to him."'

—— QUOTE ——

'I should have praised more.' (1st Duke of Wellington)

6
Historic Quotes

As with the insights from contemporary Britons set out in Chapter 5, these entries were researched from numerous archival sources. Their 'white space' presentation aims to encourage reflection of the individual entries.

Joseph Addison (1672–1719)

Essayist, poet and co-founder of the Spectator magazine

''Tis not in mortals to command success; but we'll do more, Sempronius. We'll deserve it.'

'If you wish success in life, make perseverance your bosom friend, experience your wise counsellor, caution your elder brother, and hope your guardian genius.'

Jane Austen (1775–1817)

Novelist

'It is very difficult for the prosperous to be humble.'

'We have all a better guide in ourselves, if we would attend to it, than any other person can be.'

Francis Bacon, 1st Viscount St Alban (1561–1626)

English philosopher, statesman, and essayist

'If we are to achieve results never before accomplished, we must expect to employ methods never before attempted.'

'All rising to great place is by a winding stair; and if there be factions, it is good to side a man's self whilst he is rising and to behave himself when he is placed.'

'Seek first the virtues of the mind; and other things either will come, or will not be wanted.'

'So ambitious men, if they find the way open for their rising, and still get forward, they are rather busy than dangerous; but if they be checked in their desires, they become secretly discontent, and look upon men and matters with an evil eye, and are best pleased, when things go backward.'

Joanna Baillie (1762–1851)

Poet and dramatist

'Success bestows where blessing is denied.'

Alexander Graham Bell (1847–1922)

Scientist, inventor and innovator credited with the invention of the telephone.

'The most successful men in the end are those whose success is the result of steady accretion … It is the man who carefully advances step by step, with his mind becoming wider and wider – and progressively better able to grasp any theme or situation – persevering in what he knows to be practical, and concentrating his thought upon it, who is bound to succeed in the greatest degree.'

Charlotte Brontë (1816–1855)

Novelist, poet, governess

'Men judge us by the success of our efforts. God looks at the efforts themselves.'

Robert Browning (1812–1889)

Poet and playwright

'A minute's success pays the failure of the years.'

'God will estimate success one day.'

'He ventured neck or nothing – heaven's success
Found, or earth's failure.'

Edward Bulwer-Lytton, 1st Baron Lytton (1803–1873)

Novelist, playwright, poet and politician

'The man who succeeds above his fellows is the one who early in life, clearly discerns his object, and towards that object habitually directs his powers. Even genius itself is but fine observation strengthened by fixity of purpose. Every man who observes vigilantly and resolves steadfastly grows unconsciously into genius.'

Samuel Butler (1612–1680)

Poet and satirist

'The reason why fools and knaves thrive better in the world than wiser and honester men is because they are nearer to the general temper of mankind, which is nothing but a mixture of cheat and folly, which those that understand and mean better cannot comply with, but entertain themselves with another kind of fool's paradise of what should be, not what is; while those that know no better take naturally to it, and get the start of them.'

Sir Thomas Fowell Buxton (1786–1845)

Member of Parliament, social reformer

'The road to success is not to be run upon by seven-leagued boots. Step by step, little by little, bit by bit – that is the way to wealth, that is the way to wisdom, that is the way to glory.'

Noel, 6th Baron Byron, FRS (1788–1824)

Poet and revolutionary

'Well, if I don't succeed, I have succeeded
And that's enough.'

Lewis Carroll
(pen name of The Reverend Charles Lutwidge Dodgson, 1832–1898)

Author, mathematician, logician, Anglican clergyman and photographer.

'Would you tell me, please, which way I ought to go from here?'

'That depends a good deal on where you want to get to,' said the Cat.

'I don't care much where,' said Alice.

'Then it doesn't matter which way you go,' said the Cat.

Alice in Wonderland

Sir Charlie Chaplin, KBE (1899–1977)

Actor, screenwriter, director

'I'd sooner be called a successful crook than a destitute monarch.'

George Chapman (1559–1634)

Dramatist, translator and poet

'Good success
Is oft more fatal far than bad, one winning throw,
Cast from a flattering die, may tempt a gamester
To hazard his whole fortune.'

Gilbert Keith Chesterton (1874–1936)

Journalist, novelist

'I owe my success to having listened respectfully to the very best advice, and then going away and doing the exact opposite.'

Charles Churchill (1731–1764)

Poet, political writer and clergyman

'Where he falls short, 'tis Nature's fault alone;
Where he succeeds, the merit's all his own.'

Brian Clough, OBE (1935–2004)

Footballer and football manager

'I wouldn't say I was the best manager in the business. But I was in the top one.'

'On occasions I have been big-headed. I think most people are when they get in the limelight. I call myself Big Head just to remind myself not to be.'

Samuel Coleridge-Taylor (1875–1912)

Composer

'Personally, I consider myself the equal of any white man who ever lived, and no one could change me in that respect; on the other hand, no man reverences worth more than I, irrespective of colour and creed. May I further remind the lecturer that really great people always see the best in others; it is the little man who looks for the worst – and finds it.'

Charles Caleb Colton (1780–1832)

Cleric, writer and collector

'When we fail our pride supports us and when we succeed, it betrays us.'

Sir Noel Coward (1899–1973)

Actor, playwright and composer of popular music

'Success took me to her bosom like a maternal boa constrictor.'

Quentin Crisp (1908–1999)

Author

'The formula for achieving a successful relationship is simple: you should treat all disasters as if they were trivialities but never treat a triviality as if it were a disaster.'

'If at first you don't succeed, failure may be your style.'

Samuel Daniel (1562–1619)

Poet and historian

'Th' aspirer, once attain'd unto the top,
Cuts off those means by which himself got up.'

'The Road to Success is filled with women pushing their husbands along.'
(Lord Dewar)

Sir William Davenant (1606–1668)

Poet and playwright

'In tracing human story, we shall find
The cruel more successful than the kind.'

Charles Dickens, FRSA (1812–1870)

Novelist

'Ride on! Rough shod if need be, smooth shod if that will do, but ride on!'

Benjamin Disraeli,
1st Earl of Beaconsfield, KG, PC, FRS (1804–1881)

British Conservative Statesman and Literary Figure, twice Prime Minister

'Success is the child of Audacity.' (*Islander*, Ch. 4)

'The secret of success is constancy to purpose.' (Speech, 24th June 1870)

'As a general rule the most successful man in life is the man who has the best information.'

'Whenever you see a man who is successful in society, try to discover what makes him pleasing, and if possible adopt his system.'

'Every man has a right to be conceited until he is successful.'

John Dryden (1631–1700)

Poet, playwright, literary critic

'Presence of mind and courage in distress,
Are more than armies to procure success.'

'Virtue, without success,
Is a fair picture shewn by an ill light;
But lucky men are favourites of heaven
All own the chief, when fortune owns the cause.'

'But treason is not owned when 'tis descried;
Successful crimes alone are justified.'

Dame Daphne du Maurier, Lady Browning, DBE (1907–1989)

Author of plays, novels and short stories.

'She could not separate success from peace of mind. The two must go together; her observation pointed to this truth.'

George Eliot (1819–1880)
pen name of Mary Ann Evans

Novelist

'I feel no regret that the fame, as such, brings no pleasure; but it is a grief to me that I do not constantly feel strong in thankfulness that my past life has vindicated its uses and given me reason for gladness that such an unpromising woman-child was born into the world.'

T.S. Eliot (1888–1965)

Poet, dramatist and literary critic. Nobel Prize for Literature (1948)

'Success is relative: It is what we can make of the mess we have made of things.'

Henry Fielding (1707–1754)

Novelist, dramatist and magistrate (founded the Bow Street Runners)

'A strenuous soul hates cheap success.'

'Success is a fruit of slow growth.'

Dame Margot Fonteyn de Arias, DBE (1919–1991)

Ballerina

'Great artists are people who find the way to be themselves in their art. Any sort of pretension induces mediocrity in art and life alike.'

'The one important thing I have learned over the years is the difference between taking one's work seriously and taking one's self seriously. The first is imperative and the second is disastrous.'

Elizabeth Fry (1780–1845)

Prison reformer, social reformer, philanthropist

'The rules of life:

First, – Never lose any time; I do not think that lost which is spent in amusement or recreation some time every day; but always be in the habit of being employed.

Second, – Never err the least in truth.

Third, – Never say an ill thing of a person when I can say a good thing of him; not only speak charitably, but feel so.

Fourth, – Never be irritable or unkind to anybody.

Fifth, – Never indulge myself in luxuries that are not necessary.

Sixth, – Do all things with consideration, and when my path to act right is most difficult, put confidence in that Power alone which is able to assist me, and exert my own powers as far as they go.'

'I am ready to say in the fulness of my heart, surely"it is the Lord's doing, and marvellous in our eyes"; so many are the providential openings of various kinds. Oh! if good should result, may the praise and glory of the whole be entirely given where it is due by us, and by all, in deep humiliation and prostration of spirit.'

Sir William Schwenck Gilbert (1836–1911)

Dramatist, poet and illustrator

(Ruddigore)
'If you wish in this world to advance,
Your merits you're bound to enhance;
You must stir it and stump it,
And blow your own trumpet,
Or trust me, you haven't a chance.'

'Losers visualize the penalties of failure. Winners visualize the rewards of success.'

William Gladstone (1809–1898)

*British Liberal Party statesman and
Prime Minister (1868–74, 1880–85, 1886 and 1892–94)*

'No man ever became great or good except through many and great mistakes.'

Graham Greene, OM, CH (1904–1991)

Novelist, short story writer, playwright, screenwriter, travel writer and critic

'For an artist to think in terms of success is like a priest trying to think in terms of success.'

William Havard (1710–1778)

Actor and dramatist

'Perseverance is a Roman virtue,
That wins each godlike act, and plucks success
Ev'n from the spear proof crest of rugged danger.'

William Hazlitt (1778–1830)

Writer

'As is our confidence, so is our capacity.'

'The surest hindrance to success is to have too high a standard of refinement in our own minds, or too high an opinion of the judgment of the public. He who is determined not to be satisfied with anything short of perfection will never do anything at all either to please himself or others.'

'The world judge of men by their ability in their professions, and we judge of ourselves by the same test; for it is on that on which our success in life depends.'

'The incentive to ambition is the love of power.'

'People of genius do not excel in any profession because they work in it, they work in it because they excel.'

'A gentle word, a kind look, a good-natured smile can work wonders and accomplish miracles.'

'No truly great person ever thought themselves so.'

'If you think you can win, you can. Faith is necessary to victory.'

Sir Arthur Helps (1813–1875)

Historian, novelist and essayist

'The worst use that can be made of success is to boast of it.'

Dame Barbara Hepworth (1903–1975)

Sculptor and artist

'Halfway through any work, one is often tempted to go off on a tangent. Once you have yielded, you will be tempted to yield again and again … Finally, you would only produce something hybrid.'

George Herbert (1593–1633)

Poet, orator and a priest

'The higher the Ape goes, the more he shewes his taile.'

Robert Herrick (1591–1674)

Poet

'Thus times do shift, each thing his turn does hold;
New things succeed, as former things grow old.'

Sir Alfred Hitchcock (1899–1980)

Film director and producer

'The more successful the villain, the more successful the picture.'

Margaret Hodson (1778–1852)

Author

'Bright success May only for a while sustain Man's feeble spirit.'

Aldous Huxley (1894–1963)

Writer

'Those who believe they are exclusively in the right are generally those who actually achieve something.'

'Success demands strange sacrifices from those who worship her.'

Baroness Jackson of Lodsworth (1914–1981)

Economist, writer, an early advocate of sustainable development, journalist, lecturer and broadcaster and adviser to policy-makers in the UK, and USA.

'The modern world is not given to uncritical admiration. It expects its idols to have feet of clay and can be reasonably sure that the press and camera will report their exact dimensions.'

Samuel Johnson (1709–1784)

Essayist, poet, biographer, lexicographer and a critic of English Literature.

'Life affords no higher pleasure than that of surmounting difficulties, passing from one step of success to another, forming new wishes and seeing them gratified.'

'Success produces confidence, confidence relaxes industry, and negligence ruins that reputation which accuracy had raised.'

'Disappointment, when it involves neither shame nor loss, is as good as success; for it supplies as many images to the mind, and as many topics to the tongue.'

John Maynard Keynes, 1st Baron Keynes, CB (1883–1946)

Economist

'Worldly wisdom teaches us that it is better for the reputation to fail conventionally than to succeed unconventionally.'

Lieutenant-Colonel T.E. Lawrence, CB, DSO (1888–1935)

Soldier, Writer.
Chevalier of the Legion of Honour, Croix de Guerre

'There could be no honour in a sure success, but much might be wrested from a sure defeat.'

John Lennon, MBE (1940–1980)

Rock musician, singer, songwriter, artist, and peace activist.
Founding member of 'The Beatles'.

'Woman I can hardly express,
My mixed emotion at my thoughtlessness,
After all I'm forever in your debt,
And woman I will try express,
My inner feelings and thankfulness,
For showing me the meaning of success.'

'You won't get anything unless you have the vision to imagine it.'

David Lloyd George,
1st Earl Lloyd George of Dwyfor, OM, PC (1863–1945)

*Liberal Prime Minister through the latter half of World War 1
and the first four years of the subsequent peace.*

'If you want to succeed in politics you must keep your conscience well under control.'

John Morley, 1st Viscount Morley of Blackburn, OM, PC (1838–1923)

Politician, writer and newspaper editor

'Success depends on three things: who says it, what he says, how he says it; and of these three things, what he says is the least important.'

Florence Nightingale, OM, RRC (1820–1910)

Pioneer of modern nursing 'The Lady with the Lamp', writer, statistician.

'I attribute my success to this – I never gave or took any excuse.'

Lord Olivier, OM (1907–1989)

Actor, director, producer

'Success smells like Brighton.'

John Osborne (1929–1994)

Playwright, screenwriter

'Financial success improves people who are good and debases people who are bad.'

Thomas Paine (1737–1809)

Revolutionary, radical, inventor and intellectual

'The harder the conflict, the more glorious the triumph. What we obtain too cheap, we esteem too lightly. 'Tis dearness only that gives everything its value.'

'The harder the conflict, the more glorious the triumph.'

Emmeline Pankhurst (1858–1928)

Leader of the British suffragette movement

'You have to make more noise than anybody else; you have to make yourself more obtrusive than anybody else; you have to fill all the papers more than anybody else.'

'You have to be there all the time and see that they do not snow you under, if you are really going to get your reform realized.'

Walter Pater (1839–1894)

Critic, writer and lecturer

'To burn always with this hard, gemlike flame, to maintain this ecstasy, is success in life.'

Samuel Pepys, FRS (1633–1703)

Chief Secretary to the Admiralty, Member of Parliament, Diarist

'But, Lord! To see what successe do, whether with or without reason, and making a man seem wise.' (Diary, 15th August 1666)

Alexander Pope (1688–1744)

Poet

'The race by vigour, not by vaunts is won.' (*The Dunciad*)

Beatrix Potter (1866–1943)

Children's author, illustrator, mycologist, and conservationist

'Most people, after one success, are so cringingly afraid of doing less well that they rub all the edge off their subsequent work.'

Francis Quarles (1592–1644)

Poet and prose writer

'Physicians of all men are most happy; what good success soever they have, the world proclaimeth, and what faults they commit, the earth covereth.'

Dame Anita Roddick, DBE (1942–2007)

Businesswoman (founder of the Body Shop) charity worker and campaigner.

'To succeed you have to believe in something with such a passion that it becomes reality.'

John Ruskin (1819–1900)

Art critic, social critic, author, poet and artist

'When love and skill work together, expect a masterpiece.'

'The highest reward for a man's toil is not what he gets for it but what he becomes by it.'

'Success by the laws of competition signifies a victory over others by obtaining the direction and profits of their work. This is the real source of all great riches.'

Bertrand Russell, 3rd Earl Russell, OM, FRS (1872–1970)

Philosopher, historian, logician, mathematician, Nobel Prize winner

'It seems to be the fate of idealists to obtain what they have struggled for in a form which destroys their ideals.'

'I want to say, in all seriousness, that a great deal of harm is being done in the modern world by belief in the virtuousness of work, and that the road to happiness and prosperity lies in an organized diminution of work.'

'Unless a man has been taught what to do with success after getting it, the achievement of it must inevitably leave him prey to boredom.'

Sir Walter Scott (1771–1832)

Novelist, poet and historian

The Talisman
'He that climbs the tall tree has won right to the fruit,
He that leaps the wide gulf should prevail in his suit.'

Mary Seacole (1805–1881)

Nurse. Winner of the 'Every Generation' website online poll of the 100 Great Black Britons (2004)

'Of course, had it not been for my old strong-mindedness (which has nothing to do with obstinacy, and is in no way related to it – the best term I can think of to express it being "judicious decisiveness"), I should have given up the scheme a score of times in as many days; so regularly did each successive day give birth to a fresh set of rebuffs and disappointments. I shall make no excuse to my readers for giving them a pretty full history of my struggles to become a Crimean *heroine*!'

Robert W. Service (1874–1958)

Poet

'The Sum-Up'
It is not power and fame
That make success;
It is not rank or name
Rate happiness.
It is not honour due
Nor pile of pelf:
The pay-off is: Did you
Enjoy yourself?

A pal of days gone by
I reckon more
Of a success than I
Who've gold in store
His life, though none too long,
Was never dull:
Of woman, wine and song
Bill had his full.
Friend, you are a success
If you can say:
'A heap of happiness
Has come my way.
No cheers have made me glad,
No wealth I've won;
But oh how I have had
A heap of FUN!'

Dame Edith Sitwell, DBE (1887–1964)

Poet and critic

'Put your heart, mind intellect and soul even to your smallest acts. This is the secret of success.'

'Why not be oneself? That is the whole secret of a successful appearance. If one is a greyhound, why try to look like a Pekingese?'

Frederick Edwin Smith, 1st Earl of Birkenhead (1872–1930)

Politician

'Meet success like a gentleman and disaster like a man.'

'The world continues to offer glittering prizes to those with stout hearts and sharp swords.'

Tobias Smollett (1721–1771)

Author

'What; though success will not attend on all,
Who bravely dares must sometimes risk a fall.'

Jack Solomons (1900–1979)

Boxing promoter and former fishmonger

'If you want to sell 'em fish, sell 'em big fish. That's the secret of success.'

W. Somerset Maugham, CH (1874–1965)

Playwright, novelist, and short story writer

'The common idea that success spoils people by making them vain, egotistic, and self complacent is erroneous – on the contrary it makes them, for the most part, humble, tolerant and kind. Failure makes people bitter and cruel.'

Mary Somerville (1780–1872)

Science writer and polymath, first female member of the Royal Astronomical Society. Sommerville College Oxford University named after her.

'Sometimes I find [mathematical problems] difficult, but my old obstinacy remains, for if I do not succeed today, I attack them again on the morrow.'

Herbert Spencer (1820–1903)

Philosopher

'People are beginning to see that the first requisite to success in life is to be a good animal.'

Sir Stephen Spender, CBE (1909–1995)

Poet, novelist and essayist

'In England success is supposed to be kept within the bonds of decency … to bring your friends credit for knowing you, but not pushed to that extent where they might become envious.'

Robert Louis Stevenson (1850–1894)

Novelist, poet and travel writer

'Our business in this world is not to succeed but to continue to fail, in good spirits.'

'To travel hopefully is a better thing to do than to arrive and the true success is to labour.'

'When a man loves the labour of his trade, apart from any question of success or fame, the gods have called him.'

Anthony Storr (1920–2001)

Psychiatrist and author

'It is a tragic paradox that the very qualities that have led to a man's extraordinary capacity for success are also those most likely to destroy him.'

Sir Philip Sydney (1554–1586)

Soldier, author, poet and courtier

'Who shootes at the midday Sunne, though he be sure, he shall never hit the marke; yet as sure as his is, he shall shoot higher than who ayms but at a bush.'

Alfred Tennyson, 1st Baron Tennyson (1809–1892)

Poet and Poet Laureate

'Not in the clamour of the crowded street,
Not in the shouts and plaudits of the throng,
But in ourselves are triumph and defeat.'

William Makepeace Thackeray (1811–1863)

Novelist

'One of the greatest of a great man's qualities is success; 't is the result of all the others; 't is a latent power in him which compels the favor of the gods, and subjugates fortune.'

'Do not be in a hurry to succeed. What would you have to live for afterwards? Better make the horizon your goal; it will always be ahead of you.'

Dylan Thomas (1914–1953)

Poet

'Great is the hand that holds dominion over man by a scribbled name.'

'Whatever talents I possess may suddenly diminish or suddenly increase. I can with ease become an ordinary fool. I may be one now. But it doesn't do to upset one's own vanity.'

James Thomson (1700–1748)

Poet and playwright

'It is success that colours all in life:
Success makes fools admir'd, makes villains honest;
All the proud virtue of this vaunting world
Fawns on success, and power, howe'er acquir'd.'

Sir Roy Herbert Thomson,
1st Baron Thomson of Fleet, GBE, DLitt, DCL, LLD, LHD
(1894–1976)

Newspaper and media entrepreneur

'If people knew what they had to do to be successful, most people wouldn't.'

Arnold Toynbee (1852–1883)

Economic historian and social reformer

'Do not let yourselves be discouraged or embittered by the smallness of the success you are likely to achieve in trying to make life better. You certainly would not be able, in a single generation, to create an earthly paradise. Who could expect that? But, if you make life ever so little better, you will have done splendidly, and your lives will have been worthwhile.'

'It is a paradoxical but profoundly true and important principle of life that the most likely way to reach a goal is to be aiming not at that goal itself but at some more ambitious goal beyond it.'

Anthony Trollope (1815–1882)

Novelist

'Success is the necessary misfortune of life, but it is only to the very unfortunate that it comes early.'

Unknown Author

Ladder of success

——————— 100% – I did.

——————— 90% – I will.

——————— 80% – I can.

——————— 70% – I think I can.

——————— 60% – I might.

——————— 50% – I think I might.

——————— 40% – What is it?

——————— 30% – I wish I could.

——————— 20% – I don't know how.

——————— 10% – I can't.

——————— 0% – I won't.

Sir Peter Ustinov, CBE (1921–2004)

Actor, writer, dramatist, raconteur

'People who have reached the top of the tree are only those who haven't got the qualifications to detain them at the bottom.'

Charles Wesley (1707–1788)

Leader of the Methodist movement, poet and hymn writer

'Faith, mighty faith, the promise sees,
And looks to that alone;
Laughs at impossibilities,
And cries, "It shall be done!"'

Sir PG Wodehouse, KBE (1881–1975)

Novelist, playwright, lyricist

'I attribute my whole success in life to a rigid observance of a fundamental rule – never have yourself tattooed with any woman's name, not even her initials.'

'The usual drawback to success is that it annoys one's friends so.'

Virginia Wolf (1882–1941)

Novelist and essayist

'If people are successful in their professions they lose their senses. Sight goes. They have no time to look at pictures. Sound goes. They have no time to listen to music. Speech goes. They have no time for conversation. They lose their sense of proportion – the relations between one thing and another. Humility goes.'

7
Conclusion and Success Strategies

Before compiling this book, I had thought that there might be a composite formula for success that could be derived from the pieces contributed by great Britons (in Chapter 2). There isn't and I am very surprised at the many differences between the entries (an exception being the frequent references to the Kipling poem 'If' and to Churchill quotes as inspirational). Inevitably, some words such as 'hard work' and 'perseverance' or their synonyms are used by the entrants more frequently than others but not to a significant extent (although these two attributes do feature regularly in the contemporary and historic quotations chapters). Perhaps this is because there are so many different definitions of success, as suggested in Chapter 1, or that these elements are simply 'givens'. So, I am not sure how valid an exercise it would be to compile a formula for success as part of a personal success strategy. Such a task might be better suited to reflection and review once goals have been reached. However, what might be useful is to spend some time, taking account of the views and ideas set out above and particularly the points made at the end of Chapter 2 by Dr Robert Holden, to think about what success means to you since, from such an exercise should flow the actions to achieve it and from that an eventual formula.

By the time you reach this section of the book you may anyway have formed some conclusions of your own about the concept of success, or they may have just given food for thought and some may have just made you laugh.

What I thought might be of some value in this concluding chapter is to share with you some of the material I have come across during the preparation of the book on how to achieve success. Using one of the British traits identified in the RSA 2004 study mentioned above, 'sense of humour', you might find some of these eleven outline strategies, largely American in origin, amusing and some insightful.

Firstly, a view about achieving success from the authors of *Success Built to Last*:

> '*Success Built to Last* draws on face-to-face unscripted conversations with hundreds of remarkable human beings from around the world: billionaires, CEOs, presidents of nations, Nobel laureates, celebrities and unsung heroes who've achieved lasting impact. The interviews were conducted by the authors, thought leaders in organisational development and self-improvement: "if there is one such thing as a secret we have found, this would be it: if you want success built to last, then create a life that matters (to you)." '

You may feel this is a rather wide and fairly obvious concept and if so prefer the rather more detailed approach set out by Dr David Niven in his book, *100 Simple Secrets of Successful People*, where he gives a number of clues, apparently scientifically researched, on achieving success, including:

❖ Working with people who have different opinions and approaches increases productivity an average of 14%

❖ People who speak slowly are 38% more likely to be perceived as well informed than people who speak quickly;

❖ People who volunteer for community service are 25% more satisfied with their job;

❖ 80% of CEOs say a healthy family life is crucial to a productive business life;

❖ 98% of business executives see their position as the result of plans and strategy and more than half credit their use of a successful person as an example to help define that plan.

Dr Donald Schnell gives a more practical way of finding success and believes the answer is to be found in the written word:

'I believe all success begins within you – within your mind. When you begin to create in your mind what you want and feel it, then you begin to mobilise inner and outer forces to come to your assistance. I believe that the magic of visualisation is one of the oldest secrets to successful creation on our planet. Want to make your success even more certain? Write your goal down. Brian Tracy, a peak performance expert, says that 80% of your goals will manifest on their own just by your writing the goal down. So, capture your goal on paper. Writing it down helps you to focus. Focusing makes your success more certain. Then give your visualisation fuel by feeding it with feeling. Once again, feel as if you have already attained your goal.'

Numerologists, on the other hand, argue that 'success is created through the balance and creativity of mind attracting successful conditions… Success in life should be the natural evolution of a balanced mind applying itself through Advanced Numerology.' One of the practical proposals of this doctrine is to change your name: 'A Balanced Name™ can make such a difference in creating balance, good health, and success in your life.'

Dr Wayne Dyers set out his 'ten secrets for success and inner peace' in his book of the same title, some easier to achieve in practice than others:

- ❖ Have a mind that is open to everything and attached to nothing;
- ❖ Don't die with your music still in you;
- ❖ You can't give away what you don't have (you need to possess what it is you wish to give);
- ❖ Embrace silence;
- ❖ Give up your personal history (the wake does not drive the boat forward);
- ❖ You can't solve a problem with the same mindset that created it;
- ❖ There are no justified resentments;
- ❖ Treat yourself as if you already are what you'd like to be;
- ❖ Treasure your divinity;
- ❖ Wisdom is avoiding all thoughts that weaken you.

It is interesting to compare a similar approach which is outlined by Zig Ziglar who invites readers of his book, *Success for Dummies* to 'incorporate the following things into any success strategy':

- ❖ Take a do-it-now, 'hustle' approach to life,
- ❖ Have a character base – the only one that supports long term success;
- ❖ Evaluate risks and take the best ones;

- Be a time-miser;

- Communicate effectively – both verbally and non verbally;

- Have a thick skin;

- Be an optimist and a good-finder;

- Learn to be obedient so that you can learn to lead others;

- Know that courage upholds all the other qualities;

- Be intolerant of immoral behaviour;

- Develop a sense of humour;

- Form winning habits.

A different line is suggested by Dr Robert Arnot. He points to the importance of biology to success in his book, *Biology of Success*, and argues that mental energy fuels success and he sets out 'a number of simple ways to change your life':

- Let there be light; most rooms rarely exceed 600 lux of light whereas our minds need at least 1,000 lux to begin reaping light's biological benefits;

- Let there be heat, but not too much. The optimum temperature for mental work is 70°F;

- Calm down. White noise, created by sound generators to mask more disturbing noises, can actually cause you to think of danger;

- You snooze, you lose. Getting up late on weekends and waking up early on Monday mornings can make you feel as jet lagged as if you had flown from Hawaii to New York (but without the vacation!);

- Make it smell good: Reduce anxiety levels by surrounding yourself with specific smells;

- Smile like you mean it: smiling, even if you're faking it, can make you feel better;

- Eat up: a late-afternoon carbohydrate fix can cut tension;

❖ Pump up the volume: increase the strength of your immune system by listening to the right music.

The importance of appearance and dress to achieve success is recognised by a charity which has been set up to help find work for 'disadvantaged' women.

In addition to giving women what the charity describes as 'a very pampered personal shopping experience for their interview outfit and hair and make-up training, the charity also gives women a series of further work suits that can be worn when they win their new position.'

Underpinning the work of this charity is recognition that 'a strong personal image will attract people and opportunities to you, as it increases your confidence and communication skills. It inspires loyalty and respect in your target market and establishes you as an expert in your chosen field. It is the foundation of any marketing of you. Research has shown that it takes less than 30 seconds to form a lasting impression and it can take up to 21 repeated occasions for someone to alter a disappointing first impression. So it is vital we make our first impression count.' Perhaps these ideas are applicable to a wider audience than just those facing difficulties in their lives.

The American best selling author, H. Jackson Brown Jr, sets out a strategy with *21* [worthy] *Suggestions for Success:*

1. Marry the right person. This one decision will determine 90% of your happiness or misery;

2. Work at something you enjoy and that's worthy of your time and talent.

3. Give people more than they expect and do it cheerfully;

4. Become the most positive and enthusiastic person you know;

5. Be forgiving of yourself and others;

6. Be generous;

7. Have a grateful heart;

8. Persistence, persistence, persistence;

9. Discipline yourself to save money on even the most modest salary;

10. Treat everyone you meet like you want to be treated;

11. Commit yourself to constant improvement;

12. Commit yourself to quality;

13. Understand that happiness is not based on possessions, power or prestige, but on relationships with people you love and respect;

14. Be loyal;

15. Be honest;

16. Be a self-starter;

17. Be decisive even if it means you'll sometimes be wrong;

18. Stop blaming others. Take responsibility for every area of your life;

19. Be bold and courageous. When you look back on your life, you'll regret the things you didn't do more than the ones you did;

20. Take good care of those you love;

21. Don't do anything that wouldn't make your mom proud.

If H Jackson Brown is correct in his assertion that marrying the right person is the greatest contributor to success and happiness, then ensuring a successful ongoing relationship with your partner is also key. Rachel Hall, a relationship psychotherapist featured on the BBC argues that there are seven secrets of successful relationships:

1. **Love yourself.** Unless you love yourself, it's hard for you to believe that anyone else will. Self-esteem is important for a healthy relationship. When you truly like yourself, in spite of any failings and weaknesses you may have, you'll feel confident. And when you feel confident and secure within yourself, you can enjoy being with your partner for the joy they bring to your life, not because you feel you need them to survive. If you've had bad experiences in the past, it's worth working through these issues with a trusted friend or counsellor. It can be tempting to lean on your partner and rely on them for reassurance, but the stronger you are as an individual, the stronger and more equal your relationship will be.

2. **Like your partner.** Healthy relationships happen between two people who really like each other. It may be more romantic to talk about love, but it's important to remember that love is an emotion that comes and goes. If you genuinely like each other, enjoy being together, agree with how each other thinks and behaves, and share the same dreams in life, then loving feelings will never be too far away. It's important to tell your partner you like them, too. Warm words of encouragement and support build trust and respect. Add the odd compliment as well and you'll be helping to boost their self-esteem.

3. **Make quality time.** The importance of things can be measured by the amount of time we're willing to give them. When a couple first gets together, they instinctively prioritise their relationship. But as time goes by and life gets busier with work and children, time together often slips down the list of priorities. If you don't spend regular quality time together, chances are you'll drift apart.

4. **Communicate.** Good communication is essential for a healthy relationship. It's the only way you can tell your partner who you are, what you want and why you behave the way you do. Talking is the way we let each other into our private worlds. Communicating better is about learning to say openly and honestly exactly what you think and feel. It also means listening to your partner without judgement.

5. **Argue well.** It's important to accept that arguments are a normal part of a relationship. We're all unique and so we're bound to have our differences. Couples who argue well don't have to worry about not always agreeing. A good argument is an opportunity to share your feelings and strengthen your bond by reaching a decision that you're both happy with. It can be an experience that leaves you both feeling more confident about your relationship and brings you closer together.

6. **Touch every day.** Touching is a vital human need. Studies have shown that without touching, many animals – including humans – will die in childhood. Being caressed also lowers blood pressure and releases natural opiates in the brain, as well as the chemical oxytocin, which is essential for human pair-bonding. Touch has the power to comfort and support, to protect and encourage, to relax and, of course, to arouse.

7. **Accept change.** People change over the years and it's these changes that can keep a relationship alive. Life changes too – and not always in ways that we want.

There is a British website which points to a much easier and seemingly foolproof way of achieving across the board success, by 'cosmic ordering'. It defines cosmic ordering as:

'the process of identifying something you want or need in your life and then simply placing the order with the cosmos by asking for it. Visualise what it is you want, lightly holding that request in your mind without worry or attachment to the outcome, and then releasing it to the cosmos. The cosmic ordering service should then be left to fulfil your order in its own creative way. There are many theories about how it works, but the general consensus is that at some level we are all connected; our thoughts are creative and energetic and can communicate through the cosmic connections. Whether it is our own creative thoughts, or some other power that finally manifests our desires, is a question for each individual and one of the wonderful mysteries of life.'

The website explains what is necessary in order to place successful cosmic orders:

'Be positive, be open and be at ease. Negativity, closed thinking and anxiety will kill the process dead. If you find that these things are blocking your ability to successfully place and receive your cosmic orders, then you may need to do additional clearing work to remove the emotional or psychological blocks to your success. The best thing though, is to start ordering small, inconsequential things to build your confidence in the process.'

Obviously, you will make what you will of these contributions on developing success strategies. It may well be possible to plan out a path to achievement by using some of these ideas or simply by adopting other approaches set out or implied in the chapters above. If I may I would like to leave with you one final question of my own on this topic. Can true success really be pursued? Or does it need to ensue and is it the consequence of an individual's commitment to a cause greater than themselves?

Bibliography

Peter Ackroyd (2007) *Newton*. Vintage.

Peter Ackroyd (2006) *Shakespeare, The Biography*. Vintage

Dr. Robert Arnot (2000) *The Biology of Success*. Boston, New York, London: Little Brown & Co.

Sir David Attenborough (2002) *Life on Air*. BBC Books.

John Bartlett (1992) *Bartlett's Familiar Quotations* (16th edn). Boston, Toronto, London: Little Brown and Company.

David Beckham with Tom Watt (2003) *David Beckham: My Side*. Collins Willow.

Bloomsbury Publishing Ltd. (ed.) (1988) *Who Said What When: Chronological Dictionary*. London: Bloomsbury Publishing Ltd.

Bloomsbury Thematic Dictionary of Quotations (1990) London: Bloomsbury Publishing Ltd.

Henry G. Bohn (1882) *A Dictionary of Poetical Quotations*. London: George Bell and Sons.

Marion Luna Brem (2001) *The 7 Greatest Truths About Successful Women*. New York: Berkley Publishing Group.

Steven Brindle (2006) *Brunel: The Man Who Built the World*. London: Orion Publishing Group.

Janet Browne (2003) *Charles Darwin: The Power of Place*. Pimlico.

Kevin Brown (2005) *Penicillin Man: Alexander Fleming and the Antibiotic Revolution*. Sutton Publishing.

R. Angus Buchanan (2002) *Brunel: The Life and Times of Isambard Kingdom Brunel*. London: Hambledon & London.

Sir Bobby Charlton (2007) *My Manchester United Years*. London: Headline Publishing Group.

Deepak Chopra (1994) *The 7 Spiritual Laws of Success*. San Rafael, CA: Amber-Allen Publishing.

Charlotte Church (2007) *Keep Smiling*. London: Orion.

John M Cohen (2005) *Penguin Dictionary of Quotations*. London: Penguin Books.

Jim Collins (2001) *Good to Great*. New York: Harper Collins Publishers Inc.

John Cook (1993) *The Book of Positive Quotations*. Fairview Press.

Dr. Wayne Dyers (2001) *10 Secrets for Success and Inner Peace*. Carlsbad, CA: Hay House Inc.

Leonard Roy Frank (2001) *Webster's Quotationary*. Random House.

Malcolm Gladwell (2008) *Outliers: The Story of Success*. London: Little Brown and Company.

Walter Graebner (1965) *My Dear Mister Churchill*. London: Michael Joseph.

Jonathon Green (compiler) (1982) *A Dictionary of Contemporary Quotations*. Newton Abbott, Devon: David & Charles.

John Gross (1983) *The Oxford Book of Aphorisms*. Oxford, New York: Oxford University Press.

Joel S.A. Hayward (2003) *For God and Glory: Lord Nelson and His Way of War*. US Naval Institute Press.

Christopher Hibbert (1998) *Wellington, A Personal History*. London: HarperCollins.

Robert Holden (2005) *Success Intelligence*. Hodder and Stoughton.

Antony Jay (2005) *Oxford Dictionary of Political Quotations* (3rd edn). Oxford: Oxford University Press.

Norman Jeffares & Martin Gray (eds) (1995) *Collins Dictionary of Quotations*. Glasgow: HarperCollins.

Frank Kitson (2004) *Old Ironsides: The Military Biography of Oliver Cromwell*. London: Weidenfeld & Nicolson.

Elizabeth Knowles (ed.) (1998) *Oxford Dictionary of 20th Century Quotations*. Oxford University Press.

Tim Lewens (2006) *Darwin*. Abingdon: Routledge.

Martin H. Mansel (2007) *The New Book of Business Quotations*. London: Law Pack Publishing Ltd.

Andrew Martin (2005) *Funny You Should Say That*. Penguin Books.

Paul McKenna (2007) *I Can Make You Rich*. Bantam Press.

David Meek & Tom Tyrell (2006) *Sir Alex*. Orion Books.

David Niven, PhD (2002) *100 Simple Secrets of Successful People: What Scientists Have Learned and How To Use It*. HarperSanFrancisco.

Theo Paphitis (2008) *Enter the Dragon*. Orion Books.

Elaine Partnow (1992) *The New Quotable Woman: From Eve to the Present Day*. London: Headline Book Publishing.

J Pincott (2005) *Success*. Random House.

J Porrass, S Emery & M Thomson (2007) *Success Built to Last: Creating a Life that Matters*. Wharton School Publishing.

Steven D. Price (2005) *1,001 Smartest Things Ever Said*. Guildford, CT: Lyons Press.

Gordon Ramsay (2006) *Humble Pie*. HarperCollins.

Steve Redgrave with Nick Townsend (2000) *Sir Steve Redgrave*. BBC Worldwide.

Connie Robertson (ed.) (1998) *The Wordsworth Dictionary of Quotations*. West Hertfordshire: Wordsworth Editions Ltd.

Mary Seacole (1857) *Wonderful Adventures of Mrs. Seacole in Many Lands*. London: James Blackwood.

John M. Shanahan (2005) *The Most Brilliant Thoughts of all Time*. New York: Collins.

Anne Somerset (1997) *Elizabeth I*. London: St Martin's Press.

Burton Stevenson (1974) *Stevenson's Book of Quotations* (10th edn). London: Cassell.

Jackie Stewart (2007) *The Autobiography: Winning is Not Enough*. Headline Publishing Group.

John Sugden (2004) *Nelson: A Dream of Glory*. Jonathan Cape Ltd.

Bill Swainson (ed.) (2000) *Encarta Book of Quotations*. London: Bloomsbury Publishing.

The Times Book of Quotations (Introduction by Philip Howard) (2000) Glasgow: HarperCollins.

Rhoda Thomas Tripp (1970) *The International Thesaurus of Quotations*. Penguin Books.

Michael White (1998) *Isaac Newton: The Last Sorcerer*. Fourth Estate.

Nick Williams (2003) *Unconditional Success*. Bantam Books.

Zig Ziglar (1998) *Success for Dummies*. Chicago: IDG Books Worldwide Inc.

Appendix
Your entry in a new book entitled
Great Britons On Success by Alan Coppin

This book will be published in 2009 with author's royalties being donated to the Royal Air Force Benevolent Fund, a charity which supports families of members of the Royal Air Force who are in need or distress. The publication date is to coincide with the 90th Anniversary of the RAFBF which started life in 1919, one year after the formation of the RAF.

Your support to this charity and therefore to our service personnel is requested in the form of a written contribution of up to 600 words. You will totally control your entry and I suggest the following guidelines:

1. Your name as you wish it to appear in this book, including awards, titles and honours.

2. A description of your job/position/career as you wish it to appear in the book.

3. Your personal formula for success or one you favour. Here are some examples which, hopefully, might be of some assistance:

   'Presence of mind and courage in distress are more than armies to procure success.' (JOHN DRYDEN)

   'Formula for success: under-promise and over-deliver.' (TOM PETERS)

   'Rise early; work hard; strike oil!' (J PAUL GETTY)

   'Success is going from failure to failure without loss of enthusiasm.' (CHURCHILL)

   'A=x+y+z, where A is success, x is work, y is play and z is knowing when to keep your mouth shut!' (EINSTEIN)

   'The secret of success is constancy to purpose.' (DISRAELI)

4. If you feel it necessary, a short explanation of your formula.

5. An important section setting out your own tip for success or what/who has inspired you. You might want to illustrate this point by using an anecdote. Obviously, it would be helpful if this section is insightful and original.

6. A favourite (inspirational) quotation or words from a favourite poem or song.

7. Something not covered above but which you consider fits the theme of the book!